August 1914

August 1914

Surrender at St Quentin

John Hutton

Pen & Sword
MILITARY

First published in Great Britain in 2010 by
Pen & Sword Military
an imprint of
Pen & Sword Books Ltd
47 Church Street
Barnsley
South Yorkshire
S70 2AS

Copyright © John Hutton, 2010

ISBN 978-1-84884-134-5

Typeset in 11pt Ehrhardt by
Mac Style, Beverley, E. Yorkshire

Printed and bound in the UK by CPI

Pen & Sword Books Ltd incorporates the imprints of Pen & Sword Aviation, Pen & Sword Maritime, Pen & Sword Military, Wharncliffe Local History, Pen and Sword Select, Pen and Sword Military Classics and Leo Cooper.

For a complete list of Pen & Sword titles please contact
PEN & SWORD BOOKS LIMITED
47 Church Street, Barnsley, South Yorkshire, S70 2AS, England
E-mail: enquiries@pen-and-sword.co.uk
Website: www.pen-and-sword.co.uk

Contents

'For All We Have and Are'

For all we have and are,
For all our children's fate,
Stand up and take the war.
The Hun is at the gate!
Our world has passed away,
In wantonness o'erthrown
There is nothing left to-day
But steel and fire and stone!
    Though all we knew depart,
The old Commandments stand: –
    'In courage keep your heart,
    In strength lift up your hand.'

Once more we hear the word
That sickened earth of old: –
'No law except the Sword
Unsheathed and uncontrolled.'
Once more it knits mankind,
Once more the nations go
To meet and break and bind
A crazed and driven foe.

Comfort, content, delight,
The ages' slow-bought gain,
They shrivelled in a night.
Only ourselves remain
To face the naked days
In silent fortitude,
Through perils and dismays
Renewed and re-renewed.
    Though all we made depart,
    The old Commandments stand: –
    'In patience keep your heart,
    In strength lift up your hand.'

No easy hope or lies
Shall bring us to our goal,
But iron sacrifice
Of body, will, and soul.
There is but one task for all –
One life for each to give.
What stands if Freedom fall?
Who dies if England live?

Rudyard Kipling, 1914

Acknowledgements

Many people have given me enormous help in gathering the necessary information and material to write this account of the famous 'surrender' at St Quentin. The staff of the National Archives at Kew have been unbelievably kind and patient in pointing me in the right direction and dealing with my endless requests. The same is true of the Library and Documents staff of the Imperial War Museum in London. The Museum of the Royal Regiment of Fusiliers was also a useful source of advice and help. I would like to express my profound respect and admiration to all of them.

Conor Dodd has helped me source some important eye-witness accounts and images of those tumultuous early days of the Royal Dublin Fusiliers in the First World War. Ken Anderson has been incredibly generous in allowing me to take advantage of his skills and expertise as a photographer. Toby Smart helped me in researching the sound archives of the Imperial War Museum – a treasure trove of extraordinary richness. Graham Malkin of Advanced Illustrations has done excellent work in making the maps. Robert Elkington has been gracious in allowing me to use some of his family's archive material.

Peter Scott and John Ashby have contributed so much to a fuller understanding of the events of those four days in August 1914, and their earlier accounts have laid the foundations for my own contribution to this extraordinary story. Herve Morin helped me to gain access to the records of the French Foreign Legion. To all of them I am eternally grateful.

I could not have embarked on this project, however, without the support and indulgence of my wife Heather, who has had to put up with quite a lot. She has always been willing to listen to my endless stories about the book and its progress (which I am sure I repeated over and over again). She walked the ground of Le Cateau and the retreat from Mons with me, following in the steps of Mainwaring and Elkington. She has been a wonderful source of encouragement and a tower of strength. I could not have completed this project without her.

John Hutton
London, September 2009

List of Plates

Sir Thomas d'Oyly Snow, August 1914.
Sir Tom Bridges, photographed after the war.
Brigadier-General Aylmer Haldane, August 1914.
A copy of John Elkington's 'Livret Matricule', proving that he was in the French Foreign Legion's 3e Regiment de Marche.
A copy of John Elkington's attestation papers, dated February 1915.
A copy of a medical report from Grenoble hospital, describing Elkington's leg injury.

Chapter 1

August 1914: Britain Goes to War

In our heart of hearts believing
Victory crowns the just,
And that braggarts must
Surely bite the dust,
Press we to the field ungrieving,
In our heart of hearts believing,
Victory crowns the just.

Thomas Hardy, 'Men Who March Away'

Britain began the First World War with a small professional army of well trained volunteers, although in terms of size and equipment it was, on its own, no match for its powerful opponents. Yet despite these limitations, and notwithstanding the overwhelming odds it faced, over the course of the first few hectic days of conflict the British Army renewed its formidable reputation as a highly effective military force. The battles at Mons, Audregnies, Landrecies, Elouges, Le Cateau and Nery were all marked by many individual acts of bravery and sacrifice. Indeed, in the first eight days of fighting no fewer than 16 Victoria Crosses were won by members of the British Expeditionary Force.[1] In any conflict, however, bravery always sits uneasily but inevitably alongside deeds that are less heroic. The First World War was certainly no exception. Thousands of soldiers would be court-martialled over the next four years and several hundred executed by firing squad. One of the most infamous military trials of the First World War – that of two senior infantry colonels, John Ford Elkington and Arthur Edward Mainwaring, in September 1914 – perfectly highlights this almost natural dichotomy between heroism and personal failure. The trial of these two colonels was centred, first and foremost, on the aftermath of the collision between British and German forces in late August 1914.

On 23 August 1914 the men of the British Expeditionary Force were thrown directly into the path of a force probably six times as large and yet they managed not only to avoid defeat but ultimately, in conjunction with the French Army, to turn the tide towards eventual victory. It was a close-run thing. The success of the BEF owed as much to the heroism of the troops and the individual qualities of their commanders as it did to the mistakes of their opponents. Who were these extraordinary soldiers who set off to war in August 1914?

In its structure, organisation and people, the British Army of 1914 was the mirror image of the country it served. The officer corps was recruited almost exclusively from the very top echelons of British society, while the private soldiers and NCOs came from the ranks of Britain's urban and rural poor. Scarcely educated and often in poor health, these men were subjected to a disciplined but highly paternalistic regime. Progression through and beyond the ranks was possible but extremely rare.

At the outbreak of the war British officers, as Edward Spiers[2] has pointed out, came largely from sons of the peerage and the landed gentry, from army families and from the professional classes. Public schools predominated, with their emphasis on field sports, moral discipline and loyalty all reinforcing what were rightly considered to be important military characteristics. As many as a quarter of the army's senior officers were themselves from military families, perpetuating a tradition that in many cases went back over several generations. On the whole this was, and remains, a good tradition, providing a strong sense of motivation and career direction.

Examples of this tradition can be found in the lives of nearly all the senior officers who feature in this story. Sir Tom Bridges is a case in point. Tom was born into a military family in Kent in 1872. His father was an officer in the Bengal Artillery, while his predecessors had fought with Admiral Rodney in the 'Battle of the Saints' off Dominica in 1782. Tom himself, along with one of his four brothers, joined the army in 1892 as a young and newly commissioned officer in the Royal Artillery. He would have an eventful and colourful career. In the months leading up to the war, Tom had been leading secret negotiations with the Belgian Government about British military assistance in the event of a German invasion. German operational planning was centred on a bold outflanking manoeuvre that would, in one fell swoop, cut off the Channel ports, capture Paris and encircle the French armies to the east. However, such a manoeuvre could only be executed if the German forces could wheel through Belgium on their way south. During his time on the continent Tom also indulged in a little espionage. In his memoirs, published in the inter-war years, Tom revealed some of his tricks as a spy:

> I used to spend a good deal of time at Spa [German military headquarters] or Vielsalm where a friend of ours, de Sincay, had a pack of hounds which enabled me to combine business with pleasure. For the benefit of spy-craft in general I may disclose that an expensive high powered car and a good-looking girl are the best passports to forbidden areas. Thus equipped I once visited the German camp at Elsenborn which was out of bounds, drank beer in the officers' casino and sent off a picture postcard of it to the Director of Military Intelligence.[3]

By August 1914 Tom was a major in the 4th Dragoon Guards, an Irish cavalry regiment, and would later go on to command a division on the Western Front. Eventually he was posted to lead the British military mission to the United States, once that country had joined the war in 1917. Tom Bridges had an outstanding war record and proved himself an excellent commander. He also provided one of the most compelling eye-witness accounts of the main events described later in this book.

Likewise, the two principal characters in this book both had military backgrounds. John Ford Elkington, Commanding Officer of the 1st Battalion, Royal Warwickshire Regiment in August 1914, came from a military family and was a perfect illustration of an Edwardian officer. He was born in Jamaica in 1866, the first son of Major-General J.H.F. Elkington, who was at the time a major in the 6th Regiment of Foot, soon to become the 2nd Battalion, Royal Warwickshire Regiment. He had become an officer in 1846, and had served in a number of far-flung outposts of the Empire, rising to become a General Officer in 1880. John always intended to follow in his father's footsteps. From school he went straight to Sandhurst, and after graduating joined his father's former regiment, the Royal Warwickshires, as a fresh young lieutenant in 1886. By the outbreak of the First World War, he had already served extensively with his regiment in Africa, Egypt and India, as well as during the Boer

War, where he saw active service. He assumed command of his battalion in February 1914. His career had been one of smooth and steady progression. There had been no blemish on his character or competence since his very first day as an officer. As a result, the Royal Warwickshires entered the war under the leadership of a highly experienced and capable career soldier who, on the basis of his record to date, could reasonably have expected further promotion to higher rank.

Like father, like sons. John Elkington had four brothers, all of whom became officers in the army – proof, if it were needed, that the Elkington family was very much a military one. Robert Elkington had a distinguished career in the Royal Artillery, and on the outbreak of the war took command of 40 Brigade, Royal Horse Artillery, part of 3 Division. Robert and John therefore fought briefly together during the first few days of hostilities as part of II Corps commanded by Sir Horace Smith-Dorrien, although their paths did not cross directly. In 1916 Robert became a brigadier and commanded the artillery of 56 Division. Two other brothers, Charles and George, joined the Royal Engineers and served as lieutenants. Both were to die at an early age: Charles died in Egypt in 1893 after contracting typhoid, while George died of enteric fever during the Boer War in 1901. The youngest brother, William, followed his eldest brother into the Royal Warwickshire Regiment, although John and William were destined never to serve in the same battalion at the same time. William served during the war in Gallipoli and then Mesopotamia, where he was wounded. He survived the war, and subsequently served in the Lincolnshire Regiment. He died in May 1957.

John Elkington married Mary Rew from Liverpool in 1908 and they had three children, the first son, John, being born at the family home at Purley Hall near Reading in July 1909.

John Elkington had a lot in common with Arthur Mainwaring, Commanding Officer of the 2nd Battalion, Royal Dublin Fusiliers. Also the son of a general, Mainwaring attended Poulton House School at Tangley Park near Kingston before going on to Sandhurst. Born in Jacobabad in India in 1864, the son of a major in the Jacob's Rifles (30th Native Infantry), Arthur's father had originally enlisted with the Honourable East India Company's 1st Bombay (European) Fusiliers, a regiment which would, after a number of mutations, become the Royal Dublin Fusiliers in 1881. It was therefore natural that Arthur should join his father's regiment when he left Sandhurst in 1885, a year before John Elkington. Like Elkington, Mainwaring spent most of his military career overseas, although it seems that his service during the Boer War consisted mainly of a period on the Staff rather than in the field. He took over his battalion in March 1912.

Mainwaring was more than just a professional soldier. He also had several outside interests, adding considerable depth to his character. He had published books on cards, croquet and fishing, all of them proper pursuits for the Edwardian gentleman. But he was much more than a typical Edwardian country squire. To his credit, he had also published two volumes of detailed and scholarly regimental history covering the origins of the Royal Dublin Fusiliers and their campaign in the Boer War.

Like John Elkington, Arthur Mainwaring had devoted his entire life to the army and to his regiment. He led the life of a bachelor soldier until 1912, when he married Clarice Hare in Chelsea. He was 48, his bride nearly 20 years younger. She was the widow of Lieutenant Henry Hare, late of the King's Own Yorkshire Light Infantry, who had died five years earlier. They would have no children. Mainwaring, too, could reasonably have looked forward to further promotion.

Elkington's and Mainwaring's careers in the British Army would, however, both come to a sudden and sensational end in September 1914, in perhaps one of the most famous courts martial of the First World War. They became the most senior British officers in the war to have their behaviour and conduct in the face of the enemy tested by court martial. Both were judged to have failed that test.

The court martial of Elkington and Mainwaring has, not surprisingly, been the subject of great interest and not a little mythology over the years. Sadly, not all of the published material has been universally well informed. Lynne MacDonald, who has done so much to promote a renewed popular awareness of the First World War, unfortunately managed to get some important details wrong when writing about the court martial of the two colonels.[4] In his excellent study *Mons. Retreat to Victory*, John Terraine, another outstanding scholar of the First World War, also failed to get right some important facts about Elkington. In doing so, he was probably rehashing an innocent mistake that Tom Bridges originally made in his autobiography written in the 1930s. Such mistakes have served to increase public interest and debate about the trial and its most extraordinary consequence – namely the redemption of Colonel Elkington two years later.

In addition to Tom Bridges, two other senior officers were to play a decisive role in the fate of Elkington and Mainwaring. The Royal Warwickshires under Elkington and the Royal Dublin Fusiliers under Mainwaring formed part of the 10th Infantry Brigade commanded by Brigadier-General Sir James Aylmer Haldane. Unlike Bridges, Elkington and Mainwaring, Haldane did not come from a family with a recent military connection, although some of his ancestors had certainly enjoyed high military rank. His credentials were, however, thoroughly aristocratic. He was descended from a long line of wealthy Scottish landowners from Gleneagles. His father was a doctor and his mother was the daughter of the physicist Daniel Rutherford. Haldane was commissioned into the Gordon Highlanders in 1882 and by the outbreak of the First World War had seen extensive active service both in the Boer War and in the North West Frontier Province, as well as holding senior appointments in the War Office in London.

At the beginning of the war Haldane had a good reputation in the army as an efficient and effective officer; indeed, he would go on to command first a division and later an army corps in the later stages of the war. General Sir Charles Douglas, Inspector-General of Home Forces, considered him a 'good instructor', who 'had established a good system of training in his Brigade and promises to be a thoroughly efficient Brigade commander'.[5] Major-General Sir Archibald Murray, Inspector of Infantry, who would subsequently serve as Field Marshal French's Chief of Staff, believed Haldane's 10th Brigade, along with the 13th Brigade commanded by Brigadier-General Thompson Capper, to be the best in the army. This was high praise indeed. In his autobiography written over 30 years later, Haldane himself expressed confidence that 'as far as could be judged from training in peacetime, my Brigade would give a good account of itself in the field'.[6] As it turned out, the 10th Brigade would face the harshest test of all in that first week of the war. It remains an open question whether these early positive accounts of the brigade in peacetime – certainly in relation to its command and control – were supported by what transpired in August 1914.

Despite his rapid elevation to higher rank during the course of the next two years, Haldane was not without his critics, some of whom were very high-ranking. In an interesting entry in his diary for 18 February 1916, Field Marshal Sir Douglas Haig, the Commander-in-Chief, commented on the problems he was having with Sir Herbert Plumer, then the commander of 2 Army, and remarked very unfavourably on Haldane's abilities: 'Privately I feel that Plumer is too kind to some of his subordinate commanders, who are, I fear, not fit for their appointments, eg General Haldane.'[7] Nevertheless, this jaundiced view did not stop Haig confirming Haldane's subsequent appointment that year as GOC VI Corps.

Haldane's immediate superior was Major-General Sir Thomas d'Oyly Snow, who had been appointed to the command of 4 Division in the spring of 1910. Like Haldane, Snow did not come from a military family. He was born in 1858, the first son of the Reverend George d'Oyly Snow, vicar of Blandford Forum in Dorset. Thomas enjoyed all the benefits of Victorian upper class society. He went to Eton and St John's College, Cambridge before joining the 13th Regiment of Foot in 1879. His subsequent career in the army took him all over the Empire. He served in the Anglo–Zulu War of 1879, and in various campaigns in the Sudan before returning to England to attend the newly established Staff College at Camberley. After a spell at Aldershot, Snow saw action at the Battle of Omdurman, and then served in India as second-in-command of the 2nd Battalion, Northamptonshire Regiment.

Snow was intensely proud of 4 Division, and by the outbreak of the war he felt that it could be 'put down as having arrived at as high a state of efficiency as is possible in peace but we were terribly short in numbers and the restrictions as to training ground cramped the important study of ground. Still, the training of officers had reached a high level and there were sufficient NCOs and men trained to leaven the reservists when they arrived.'[8] He was more than satisfied with his brigade commanders, believing them to be 'far and away better than the brigadiers of other divisions. I knew their ways and they knew mine.'[9]

Snow was particularly impressed with Haldane. In December 1913 he had described him as 'one of the most energetic officers both mentally and physically whom I have ever met. He is a first class instructor in all stages of training, an excellent commander in the field with a quick eye for country and a situation and can rapidly apply his deep study of military history to the task in hand. He is very methodical and has had a unique experience in both the office and the field. He has the confidence of his subordinates and I am fortunate in having in him a brigade commander I can put absolute trust as regards loyalty and action.'

Unfortunately, however, this high opinion was not reciprocated. Snow's rosy view of his brigade commanders was not universally reflected in the brigadiers' own perceptions of Snow himself. Haldane in particular was critical of Snow's overall command of the division and his abilities as a tactician. He felt that Snow lacked tactical judgement as well as boldness in command. In May 1913 he wrote that Snow 'again showed his ignorance of any tactical principles and had we not been fighting an imaginary enemy we should certainly have been beaten; as it was the fight was considered drawn, whereas by massing against the enemy's nearest flank he could have been routed. General Snow ignored the principle of economy of force, of direction, the mass and security. He was, however, quite pleased with himself.'

Such strong criticism of his commanding officer could hardly bode well for the future command of the division once military operations in France began in earnest. Haldane's savage words, however, need to be put in context. In the annual manoeuvres of 1912, the last major training exercise before the war started, Snow was part of the winning side against the forces commanded by Douglas Haig. Haldane's criticism of Snow's prowess as a commander may therefore have been a little wide of the mark. There is also nothing to suggest that Snow was aware of the criticism of his abilities as a commander that swirled around within his own division as it set off to war in August 1914. As far as the outside world could tell, 4 Division was ready for war. Exactly how ready was a moot point, and this was particularly true of the staff. Upon mobilisation, each of the divisional staffs was rapidly expanded to six officers, and as a result the staffs were flooded by a motley crew of inexperienced individuals. According to Sir James Edmonds, Snow's chief staff officer in 1914, the new arrivals who joined the staff of 4 Division were either incompetent or totally unsuited to staff work. The officer with the most qualifications, an instructor at Camberley, was a complete novice at staff duties. In his memoirs Edmonds recounted: 'He could not write a practical, only an academic operation order; had never heard of a sliding time scale for marches, and knew nothing of the routine of preparing simultaneously sufficient copies of an order and of a march table. In fact in the first days, he was a hindrance rather than a help.'[10]

Snow enjoyed rapid promotion to lieutenant-general once the war started, and went on to command VII Corps, part of Allenby's Third Army, from 1915 until the close of the Battle of Cambrai in late 1917, at which point, with his health worsening, he asked to be relieved of his command. Snow will perhaps be most remembered for his conduct of the disastrous attack at Gommecourt on the opening day of the Battle of the Somme, where appalling casualty rates in his two attacking divisions, combined with a complete failure to reach any of the objectives for the assault, led to serious – and justifiable – recriminations amongst the higher command. Snow endured heavy criticism for what was, after all, intended to be a purely diversionary operation designed to confuse the German High Command about the focus of the main British effort, thus preventing any reinforcement of the Somme front itself. The attack at Gommecourt was heroically prosecuted by the troops, but it turned out to be a forlorn and suicidal assault. In a strange echo of pre-war events, much of the criticism aimed at Snow originated from some of his subordinate officers. Major-General Arthur Holland, commanding Third Army's artillery during the fighting at Gommecourt, tried to persuade Allenby to sack General Snow because of the 'monstrously bad' planning of the attack. Snow himself was quite pleased with the attack at Gommecourt. In a diary entry on 4 July, he wrote, 'I was quite content with my show. I think if things are kept humming on all fronts as they are now the war cannot last long ...'. His evident lack of appreciation of the real situation on the ground underlines some of the concerns Haldane expressed in 1913 about his superior officer's qualities as a commander.

Irrespective of the personal strengths and weaknesses of particular officers, the British Army itself had undergone significant change in the years leading up to the First World War. Reform had started as early as 1871, when the old army of the peninsular campaign began to be replaced by an army organised along recognisably more modern lines. The British Army had not, however, moved towards becoming a genuine, open meritocracy as we would understand that concept today. In truth, this would have been impossible in the circumstances prevailing in Britain at the time. No part of British society in the Edwardian era shared any of the characteristics of an open meritocracy, and it would be unrealistic to expect the army to have been any different.

Nevertheless, the reforms begun in the 1870s had been profound. By the time the war started in 1914, officers were no longer allowed to purchase their own commissions – an important and significant milestone on the road towards creating a truly professional army – although personal wealth was a useful bonus given the expenses associated with mess life. Thus there was, at least to some extent, the requirement for merit to be considered when it came to promotions. It is therefore possible to claim that at the outbreak of the war the officer corps was, by and large, better trained and better prepared for war than at any time in its history. Elkington and Mainwaring can be considered as products of this new professionalism that emerged after the inadequacies and failures exposed by the South African campaign.

Other reforms had also been introduced to support this momentum towards a more professional army. A General Staff was constituted in 1904 to act as the 'brains of the British Army'.[11] Instruction for officers of all branches of the staff was provided at the new Staff College at Camberley, which was greatly enlarged.

Whatever its social composition, the British Army of 1914 was not an organisation lacking in military experience. Officers like Snow, Haldane, Bridges, Elkington and Mainwaring had all fought in a number of expeditionary campaigns and could all be considered seasoned professionals with extensive operational experience. But it was not exactly the sort of experience that could easily be translated into the campaign of 1914 and the horrors of modern warfare on an industrial scale against a technologically comparable opponent. As Nikolas Gardner[12] has commented, the 1914 campaign would prove to be unprecedented in its scale and intensity. Until 1914 the principal task of the British Army had been to police the Empire, dealing with often poorly equipped and badly organised insurrections, where the outcome was inevitable. No serving British Army officer in 1914 had faced an enemy as well equipped, well trained and well resourced as the German Army. As a result, and not entirely unsurprisingly, the first few weeks of the war placed a unique strain on every man serving in the British Expeditionary Force, senior officers as well as other ranks. Snow, Haldane, Bridges, Elkington and

Mainwaring and the men under their command would prove to be no exceptions. How each was to come through this ordeal of fire will be the focus of later chapters.

In the years preceding the outbreak of hostilities, Britain had been fortunate in having an outstanding Secretary of State for War in R.B. Haldane, who had done the very best he could with the insufficient resources provided for defence by the Liberal Government. Haldane wanted a more proficient force, with its regulars forming a 'sharp point of finely tempered steel', a Special Reserve that could be rapidly mobilised to provide immediate replenishment, and a new Territorial Force to provide the foundations for a much larger army that could, if necessary, take on its most obvious potential adversary – Germany. Largely because of Haldane's clear leadership, and his wise choice of military advisers in the form of Gerald Ellison and Douglas Haig, Britain was able to deploy a highly capable army into the field of European operations in August 1914. Divided initially into two corps, each consisting of two infantry divisions and a cavalry division, the British Expeditionary Force collided heavily with the advancing German Army at Mons on 23 August and again at Le Cateau three days later. Despite being massively outnumbered, the BEF inflicted heavy losses on the enemy as it sought to manoeuvre into better positions in closer proximity to the neighbouring but rearward forces of General Lanrezac's Fifth French Army. Few would disagree with the view of the author of the *Official History of the Great War*, General Edmonds, that 'in every respect the Expeditionary Force of 1914 was incomparably the best trained, best organized and best equipped British Army that ever went forth to war'.[13] But the truth remains that it was not particularly well equipped or trained to fight the type of war it found itself fighting.

Although obliged to cede ground in the face of the overwhelming German onslaught, the BEF nonetheless managed to conduct a skilful withdrawal, despite being outgunned and outnumbered. It would, eventually, turn the tide of the German advance across France. But it cannot be said that the two battles at Mons and Le Cateau and the subsequent retreat followed a perfectly planned and executed strategy – they did not. In any case, such things are rare in warfare. There was an element of panic and confusion surrounding all of these events. Luck would also play its part in allowing the BEF to avoid defeat. So too would errors made by the German commanders. The fog of war began to thicken almost immediately after the first shot was fired. Plans collapsed under the weight of events, and there were problems in communicating between units. Officers at all levels found themselves having to extemporise with little knowledge of what was going on around them. Command and control at divisional, brigade and battalion level were all adversely affected, particularly on 26 August at Le Cateau. This was, after all, a battle that had started without the express agreement of the Commander-in-Chief and at very short notice, and therefore the men had little time to prepare defensive positions while officers struggled to send effective orders to units in the front line. To make matters even worse, both British flanks were in the air from the very start of the fighting. It is this chaotic situation that forms the extraordinary backdrop to the court martial of Elkington and Mainwaring in September 1914.

The purpose of this narrative is to recount how each of the principal characters dealt with the strain imposed on their physical and mental resources as officers in the first few cataclysmic days of the British campaign in France in 1914, and to expose how this seriously affected the commands with which they had been entrusted. For Elkington and Mainwaring, it would culminate not only in the abrupt termination of their distinguished careers in the British Army, but in the casting of a long shadow over their character and good name. In Mainwaring's case the shadow would never be truly lifted. But the final chapter in Elkington's quite extraordinary career would end on a much more positive note as he deservedly recovered his good name and reputation through his undoubted personal bravery as a soldier, not in the British Army but in that of its closest ally, France.

For General Haldane, the first few days of the war made a profound impression on his view of the campaign. This was hardly surprising, given that his brigade largely disintegrated as a coherent unit on its first contact with the enemy, and as a consequence his ability to exercise command would turn out to be extremely limited. His frustration with his battalion commanders was also palpable. But his career would remain unaffected by the events at Le Cateau and its aftermath, and he would emerge free from any personal blame or criticism. The same can be said of General Snow. Bridges came through it all as something of a heroic swashbuckling cavalier: he was involved in a series of cavalry charges and gallops in four days of fire and manoeuvre, but insisted on a strict code of gentlemanly behaviour among his fellow officers.

In recounting these events, I have tried not to take sides or to point the finger of blame. In any event, guilt or innocence cannot now be established with any absolute clarity or certainty because the historical audit trail does not allow for this. Only a few pieces of documentary evidence relating to the court martial of Elkington and Mainwaring are left for us to peruse. The verdict of the court martial was, in any case, not a statement of legal facts or principles, but rather the subjective opinion of their fellow officers on their behaviour. Interestingly, some of the most senior officers involved took a very different and far less critical view of the events that brought Elkington's and Mainwaring's careers in the British Army to an end. Certainly, the actions of both men are capable of a number of different interpretations, some favourable, some not. This is far from being a simple case of right or wrong.

But although the verdict of the court martial is clear, the verdict of history is an altogether different matter. It is clearly impossible to change the court's verdict or to somehow pardon these two officers for the offences they were held to have committed. The verdict of their fellow officers will stand for all time as the definitive contemporary judgement on the actions of Elkington and Mainwaring over those four decisive days in late August 1914. But justice is a restless commodity, not easily satisfied merely by the adherence to form or process. For all who share an interest in understanding this extraordinary period in our nation's history, the fate of Elkington and Mainwaring remains a compelling story, and one that we should all be free now to consider for ourselves. It is not simply a story about the behaviour of two senior officers. It is the story of an army under pressure and how it reacted to the enormous strains of a new kind of warfare conducted on an unprecedented scale and with unprecedented violence.

It is, however, impossible to avoid the conclusion that mistakes were made by these two officers and that their personal judgement became clouded, no doubt largely because of the conditions that prevailed during those four quite extraordinary days in August. The confusion was caused by a lack of information regarding the whereabouts of the enemy as well as their own forces. Physical exhaustion and mental fatigue played their part too. The anger and frustration expressed by their senior commanders, particularly General Haldane, at the turn of events at Le Cateau and during the shambolic retreat to St Quentin in those scorching hot days of August 1914 are also apparent. Reputations were on the line. And, as subsequent developments made clear, it was not just the reputations of the individuals concerned that were at stake. So too was the view history would take of the overall conduct of the British Army during this crucial period in the war.

Chapter 2

23–25 August:
Elkington and Mainwaring Go to War

Where are the lads of the village tonight?
Where are the nuts we knew?
In Piccadilly – in Leicester Square?
No, not there. No, not there.
They're taking a trip on the continon',
With their rifles and their bayonets bright,
Facing danger gladly, where they're needed badly,
– That's where they are tonight.

from a popular song

On 4 August 1914 the headquarters of Haldane's 10 Infantry Brigade, part of 4 Division under General Sir Thomas d'Oyly Snow, was at Shorncliffe Camp near Folkestone in Kent. In addition, three of the brigade's four battalions were based there, including Elkington's Royal Warwickshires. The Royal Dublin Fusiliers were based at Gravesend. Like other units of the army, the division had been placed on alert status via a telegram sent from London on 29 July, issued under War Office plans for general mobilisation. By the end of July Austria and Russia had both begun to mobilise, followed on 1 August by both France and Germany. War between the great powers of continental Europe now looked inevitable.

On receipt of this precautionary warning from the War Office, units of the division, including the battalions of 10 Brigade, were sent to man various coastal defences, including those at Dover, Sheerness and Harwich, against the risk of invasion, until Territorial units could be brought in to replace them. There was something of a theatrical dimension to these deployments as the Royal Navy was in a good position both to deter and prevent any such landings. But it was probably good for local morale, if nothing else. A composite battalion formed from the three battalions stationed at Shorncliffe was dispatched to the Isle of Sheppey for the same reason, as it was thought that this area was well suited to a hostile landing. The adjutant of this ad hoc formation was none other than 27-year-old Bernard Montgomery, then a young lieutenant in the 1st Battalion, Royal Warwickshire Regiment. He wrote to his mother on 30 July telling her, 'We have a great many posts out on the shore round about and have to be constantly on the lookout. I think it is just a precautionary move so as not to be caught napping.'[14]

Through the early summer of 1914 Generals Snow and Haldane had been heavily involved in planning the annual training manoeuvres for the division and the Territorial battalions associated with it. These plans were quickly put on hold and the exercises were cancelled on 2 August, the same day that the British Government learned of Germany's request for unimpeded passage for its army through neutral Belgium. If mobilisation were to proceed in accordance with the carefully drawn up plans of the War Office, the Territorial units needed to be at their peacetime stations. These training manoeuvres would therefore only serve to impede Britain's transition to full wartime conditions.

On 3 August Germany declared war on France and the next day on Belgium. Having promised to preserve Belgian neutrality, Britain herself was drawn into the war at 11pm on 4 August. The die was cast. The most catastrophic war in the history of the world had begun.

A few years earlier a scheme had been developed under which Britain was to send military assistance to France in the event of war. The scheme was the brainchild of General Sir Henry Wilson, who from 1907 to 1910 had been Commandant of the new Staff College set up by the new Liberal Secretary of State for War, R.B. Haldane. From 1910 until the outbreak of war Wilson had been Director of Military Operations at the War Office and had worked closely with his French counterparts in developing a new plan for the British Army to act in concert with the French in defeating a German attack on Britain's new Entente ally. The army was reorganised by Haldane into an expeditionary force to counter just this eventuality. The plan involved the dispatch of up to six infantry divisions and one cavalry division to an area between Avesnes and Le Cateau, with the British Expeditionary Force taking up a position on the left flank of the French Army as it moved to meet the German advance through Belgium.

Alternatively, if six infantry divisions could not be spared, four would be sent immediately (within the first 16 days), with another two joining them later. Under this scenario, the latter two divisions would be retained for home defence, protecting the UK from the threat of invasion, until they could be replaced through the mobilisation of Territorial units. Pending the final determination of these issues, 4 Division began the job of mobilising for war. Large numbers of reservists began to arrive at Shorncliffe and Gravesend to join the battalions of 10 Brigade, as the country responded to the call to arms. The BEF would rely heavily on the reserve to make up its wartime strength. Infantry battalions were largely under-strength in August 1914 and had in their ranks many young soldiers and recruits who were not fully trained and therefore unable to go to war anyway.

Although the BEF is rightly described as a force of regular soldiers, this creates rather a false impression of the real situation in many of its infantry battalions. In truth, it was made up of a large number of reservists who had only just returned to the army when Britain mobilised for war. Not all these men were perfectly fit, nor had they yet fully adjusted back into regimental life. Many would struggle to cope with the physical conditions they encountered in France, especially during the arduous advance to Mons and the subsequent retreat. As with all military campaigns, little details often assumed epic significance. In 1914 the new boots issued to the Reservists would emerge as a frequent cause of complaint. The new leather was hard and rough, so that marching became a painful business; given the amount of marching that lay ahead, these badly fitting boots rapidly became the bane of many a reservist's life in the critical first few days of the war. One of these reservists was Private R. Hill, who reported to the Royal Warwickshires' regimental depot on 5 August:

> What a meeting of old friends! All were eager to take part in the great scrap which every pre-war soldier had expected. At the depot all was bustle but no confusion. In the mobilisation stores, every Reservist's arms and clothing were ticketed and these were soon issued with webbing equipment. About 300

men were then selected and warned to hold themselves in readiness to proceed to the South Coast to make up the war strength of the battalion stationed there. There was great competition to go with this draft ...[15]

On 5 and 6 August the Cabinet met to decide on its plans to embark the BEF for operations in France. Haldane was already aware that his brigade might be retained temporarily in the UK for the purposes of home defence,[16] so the telegrams that arrived at Shorncliffe on the morning of 7 August probably came as no surprise. The Cavalry Division, along with 1, 2, 3 and 5 Divisions would go out to France immediately, while 4 and 6 Divisions would stay at home for the present. In order to lessen the chances of a German landing interfering with the dispatch of the BEF, the new Secretary of State for War, Lord Kitchener, decided to send two infantry brigades from 4 Division to Cromer and York. Orders were received for 10 Brigade to move immediately to York, with the first train leaving Shorncliffe at 1.20am on 8 August. The whole operation had to be improvised, with its stated objective being the protection of the Yorkshire coast and the ports of Middlesbrough and the Tees estuary.

Having arrived in York at 9am, the officers spent several hours trying to find suitable accommodation for their men. Two battalions of the brigade, 2nd Seaforth Highlanders and 1st Royal Irish Fusiliers, travelled north to Darlington to help prepare the north-eastern coast against potential German attacks. The Royal Warwickshires and the Royal Dublin Fusiliers remained in York, being billeted over the next few days partly in the main stand at the racecourse, with others lodging at GNER premises in the city centre.

Nothing of note happened to these two battalions while they were stationed in York, although they were doubtless made welcome by civic dignitaries and local people. The Germans did not make an appearance. Back in July the Royal Navy had assembled an enormous fleet of warships to practise war mobilisation procedures in home waters, and their presence in the North Sea put paid to any prospect that Germany would even consider attempting to land troops in Britain. However, the battalions' presence in the city doubtless generated public interest and attention, as well as offering some reassurance to the population. The men would have continued to train energetically, but for most of them their time in Yorkshire would have been a distraction from the serious business of getting ready to join the fighting in France. For Private Hill, at least, this period in Yorkshire had been put to proper effect:

> After a fortnight's strenuous training in Yorkshire … we had welded together and were a really fine body of men, hard as nails, average age about 25 and every man with the idea that he was equal to three Germans. Splendid men, enthusiastic and brave, and going to fight, they thought, for a righteous cause.[17]

Tom Bridges, in the meantime, had already been sent across the Channel to France with 2 Cavalry Brigade, arriving in Boulogne with his regiment the day after 10 Brigade was sent to York. He recalled:

> Having a whole Sunday to kill there before we could entrain for the front we took the regiment down to Hardelot and bathed men and horses. Returning from the sea we were surprised to find two French batteries of 75s [coming into] action against us in the sand-hills flanked by their sweating and blowing teams. The Commandant told us that we had been reported as a hostile landing.[18]

Within a few days the War Office finally made the decision to send 4 Division to France to join the BEF. On 18 August the men moved by train to Harrow, where 10 Brigade encamped on Harrow Weald Park, with the divisional headquarters at the Kings Head Hotel in Harrow itself. Bernard Montgomery recalled later in his memoirs some of the advice Elkington gave him at this time:

> The CO said that in war it was advisable to have short hair since it was then easier to keep it clean; he had all his hair removed with the clippers by the regimental barber and looked an amazing sight. Personally I had mine cut decently by a barber in Folkestone. Being totally ignorant about war I asked Elkington if it was necessary to take any money with me. He said money was useless in war as everything was provided for you. I was somewhat uncertain about this and decided to take

ten pounds with me in gold. Later I was to find this invaluable
and was glad I had not followed his advice about either hair or
money.[19]

Montgomery might not have taken Elkington's advice on either of these
subjects, but nor did he ever voice any criticism in his memoirs or
elsewhere of Elkington's judgement or behaviour as his commanding
officer during the brief time they fought together in France.

Snow recalled the time spent by the division at Harrow:

We spent the time route marching, and before we left the
Reservists really began to get into shape and I was very thankful
that we had had those few days to get feet and boots in order
instead of being rushed overseas like the other four divisions
had been. It made all the difference to us later.[20]

On 19 August Sir John French, Commander of the BEF, was notified that
4 Division would be sent immediately to join the ranks of the British
Army in France.

The division's artillery units left first. On the evening of 21 August
Captain Pusey, serving with 31 (Howitzer) Battery, XXXVII Brigade,
Royal Field Artillery, marched proudly and noisily with his guns, limbers
and wagons through the streets of Willesden to the goods station at Royal
Oak. He recalled: 'We sang "Tipperary" and "Who's your lady friend?"
as we marched.'[21]

On 22 August 4 Division's infantry battalions left Harrow to join the
war. In the early hours the headquarters of 10 Brigade, together with the
Royal Warwickshires and the Royal Dublin Fusiliers, all arrived in
Southampton, where they boarded the SS *Caledonia* of the Blue Anchor
Line bound for Boulogne. It was an uneventful crossing. Royal Navy
escorts provided protection from any possible hostile German naval forces
for the *Caledonia* and her passengers and the ship berthed safely at 8pm
that evening. The men stayed on board overnight, where they were fed
and could sleep reasonably comfortably. Disembarkation began at 4.30am
the following morning.

Private Hill of the Royal Warwickshires described the scene that
greeted the men as they disembarked:

What a contrast between us and the slipshod, undersized French Territorials who were guarding the docks. In their baggy red trousers and long blue coats they looked like comic-opera soldiers! We looked smart in our new khaki, and training had made us broad chested and clean looking. We marched through the narrow streets of Boulogne singing popular songs. The enthusiasm of the French people was unbounded. They broke our ranks to shower gifts upon us and many a blushing Tommy was kissed by men and women.[22]

The movement of the division to France had gone exceptionally smoothly, even though it was a huge logistical operation involving 73 trains and several steamers. Of his journey across the Channel Snow recalled:

the only hitch was that the vessel HQ Staff of the Division crossed in was so light and therefore high out of the water that the cranes were not high enough or the chains long enough to be able to load her. The stores earmarked for that ship had to go on another which caused some confusion.[23]

The war itself had started in earnest the very morning of their arrival in France. The first outbreak of serious fighting between the British and German Armies at Mons had started at around 6am, at roughly the same time that elements of 10 Brigade began assembling on the quayside and took their first steps on French soil. Elkington's and Mainwaring's battalions formed up at the quayside and were marched away to tented camps at Temporary Camp Number 3 on the outskirts of the town near the Colonne de la Grande Armée. The citizens of Boulogne, especially the young women, gave the men a warm and enthusiastic welcome.

Corporal O'Donnell, serving in D Company of the Royal Dublin Fusiliers under Captain Higginson, recalled the first few hours the men spent in Boulogne:

... we marched from the boat through the town to the rest camp singing all the way. The town was beautifully decorated. The whole population of the town came up around our camp and

presented everyone, including the officers, with a small
tricolour which we stuck behind our cap badges.[24]

Buttons and badges and many other items of equipment were freely
traded. Here the men stayed until the evening. At 7pm the Royal
Warwickshires and the Royal Dublin Fusiliers paraded and then marched
back to Boulogne where four trains were waiting to take them towards the
front.

There can be no doubt that 23 August was a long, gruelling day for the
newly disembarked men of 10 Brigade, not least because the weather was
hot and fine. The Royal Warwickshires were the first to leave the city, at
11.30pm, followed half an hour later by the Royal Dublin Fusiliers on the
second of the trains taking the brigade to its final destination. The
division was bound for Le Cateau, via Amiens and St Quentin, and the
first troops began to arrive there at around 10am on 24 August.

In contrast, Tom Bridges' progress towards the front had been very
different:

> We detrained at Hautmont and marched north in triumphal
> procession, roses all the way, feted and cheered by the
> unfortunate inhabitants who were so soon to see our backs in
> full retreat and themselves abandoned. The weather was so
> perfect and the country looked so peaceful and prosperous that
> it was difficult to imagine that we were not merely taking part
> in some new form of international manoeuvres.[25]

Priority had been given to getting 4 Division's infantry units up to the
fighting area as quickly as possible. By the morning of 24 August no fewer
than 11 battalions of infantry plus several units of artillery had arrived at
Le Cateau – a not inconsiderable feat of logistics. It had been decided,
however, by the War Office that the division's signals and cavalry
reconnaissance units, together with various other supporting elements,
would be sent to France later. This would have serious consequences over
the next few critical days. In particular, it meant that 4 Division would
have no 'eyes and ears' to help protect it as it moved, frequently at night
and over unfamiliar terrain, against an enemy whose whereabouts were
often unclear.

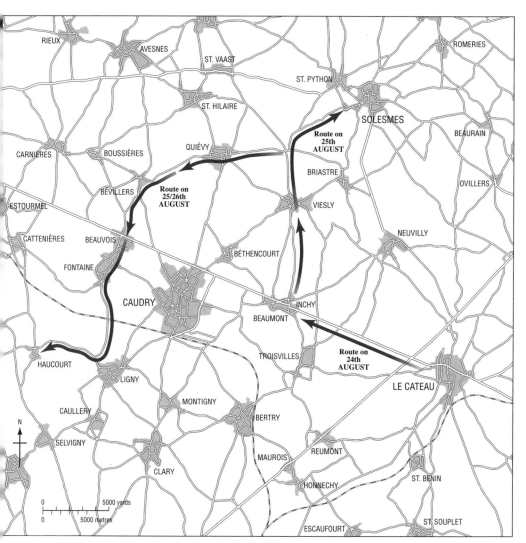

The movements of the 1st Battalion, Royal Warwickshire Regiment and the 2nd Battalion, Royal Dublin Fusiliers, 24–26 August 1914.

On arrival at Le Cateau, the division was ordered to move forward to take up positions around Solesmes, a key road junction 8 miles to the north, and to form a rearguard to assist the retirement of Sir Horace Smith-Dorrien's II Corps from the battlefield at Mons. This corps, consisting of 3 and 5 Divisions, together with 19 Brigade, had borne the brunt of the German attack and had suffered over 1,600 casualties.

General Snow was immediately taken for a briefing by the staff of GHQ at Le Cateau:

> The situation was immediately explained to me by my dear old friend Henry Wilson, who was Deputy Chief of Staff, in that half chaffing, half serious way which was peculiar to him. I gleaned that 3 and 5 Divisions had been retreating and fighting for 36 hours and that they had had about as much as any troops could stand and GHQ feared that one little more push and they might be over the brink and the retreat would become a rout. I also gathered that I was, as soon as I could collect enough troops, to push north and intervene between the enemy and the hard-pressed 3 and 5 Divisions and cover their retreat even if my division got decimated in doing so.[26]

It was a rude awakening for the men of 4 Division. Owing to the exposed position of the BEF at Mons – it was several miles in front of its nearest French neighbours on the right and protected only by weak French Territorial divisions on its left – Sir John French, in the early hours of 24 August, had ordered I and II Corps to retreat about 8 miles southwards to a new east–west line running from La Longueville (a village 5 miles to the west of the fortress town of Maubeuge) westward through Bavai and 4 miles beyond it to the hamlet of La Boiserette. All in all, this would create a front some 7 miles long. French had originally intended to stand his ground and fight it out at Mons, which was also Henry Wilson's initial instinct. But with both of the BEF's flanks largely unprotected and large enemy forces to the front as well as to the sides, this would have been courting disaster, especially when news reached the British commanders at Mons of French retirements on the right.

The British had come into contact with a vastly superior German force at Mons, and now had the job of extracting themselves from a dangerous

situation, while keeping their options open for the future. It had
necessarily taken time for the BEF to assemble as a fighting force in
France and then to move forward to engage the enemy. While the British
and French were getting ready for hostilities, the Germans had pushed an
enormous number of troops through Belgium in order to outflank the
French and British Armies in the north and encircle the larger French
forces to the south and east. On the German right wing were three great
armies, the First Army under von Kluck, the Second Army under von
Bulow and the Third Army under von Hausen. They had a combined
strength of 750,000 men. Facing them were Lanrezac's Fifth Army of
254,000 men and the BEF of just over 100,000 men. If Sir John French
had decided to stand and fight, it is clear that I and II Corps of the BEF
would have been annihilated.

At Mons, I and II Corps had been attacked by four corps of infantry
and a cavalry corps. Most of this force had been directed at II Corps,
while I Corps had hardly been involved at all in the day's fighting. The
troops under Haig's command incurred only a handful of casualties on 23
August. They had taken up positions on the right flank of II Corps, facing
east. The full force of the German advance had come straight at Smith-
Dorrien's men as they lined the banks of the Mons Canal. During the
evening I Corps was thus able to retire almost completely without
interference.

There was another good reason for French to pull back. The position
at Mons was a poor one to defend, even had the BEF not been so
comprehensively outnumbered. Both 3 and 5 Divisions were stretched
out along a 15-mile front on the south side of the Mons–Conde Canal,
which itself formed a hook around Mons, creating an unwelcome and
awkward salient. This salient rapidly became a dangerous Achilles' heel
for the defenders as the German attack developed. Troops in this little
pocket were attacked from three sides, making it almost impossible to
hold. But if the salient around the canal to the north of Mons could not
be defended, the entire British position would be at risk. This is precisely
what happened as the German attack gathered momentum.

To make matters worse, the approaches to the north were also obscured
by numerous houses and small hamlets as well as slag heaps, factories and
other urban obstacles. The troops lining the canal had very poor visibility
over the opposite bank. Nor was the canal the natural defensive position

it might at first have seemed. It was not particularly deep or wide, and there were 18 bridges over its 15-mile length, creating extra pressure on the defenders at those sites. There was no doubt that a determined enemy would sooner or later be able to force a crossing with relative ease somewhere along this long and exposed front, turning the flanks of the defenders and getting in behind the lines of those in the front rank.

For the British, the battle turned out to be one in which the rifle predominated. Their well aimed and rapid rifle fire took a terrible toll on the massed ranks of the advancing German infantry once the main assault was launched in the early hours of the morning, as many personal accounts bore witness. One British NCO later observed that, 'They were in solid square blocks, standing out sharply against the skyline. And you couldn't help hitting them. They seemed to stagger like a drunk man hit suddenly between the eyes. After which they made a run for us, shouting some outlandish cry that we couldn't make out ...'.[27] A private in the Gordon Highlanders provided an even more graphic account of the slaughter:

> Poor devils of infantry. They advanced in companies of 150 men in files five deep and our rifle has a flat trajectory of 600 yards. Guess the result. We could steady our rifles on the trench and take deliberate aim. The first company were simply blasted away to heaven by a volley at 700 yards and in their insane formation every bullet was almost sure to find two billets. The other companies kept advancing very slowly using their dead comrades as cover but they had absolutely no chance ...[28]

Corporal William Holbrooke of 4 Royal Fusiliers, at the apex of the salient formed by the canal around Mons, witnessed at first hand the first few hours of the fighting:

> Bloody Hell! You couldn't see the earth for them there were that many. Time after time they gave the order 'rapid fire'. Well you didn't wait for the order really. You'd see a lot of them coming in a mass on the other side of the canal and you just let them have it. They kept retreating and then coming forward and then retreating again. Of course, we were losing men and

lots of the officers, especially when the Germans started this shrapnel shelling and they had machine guns – masses of them. But we kept flinging them back.[29]

As Corporal Holbrooke suggests, the battle at Mons offered an opportunity for the Germans to demonstrate their superiority over the British in artillery and they took full advantage. For the defenders it would prove to be an extremely uncomfortable experience. One of the soldiers who endured the enemy artillery fire that day wrote to *The Times* with this account of the German barrage:

> We were in the trenches waiting for them but we didn't expect anything like the smashing blow that struck us. All at once, so it seemed, the sky began to rain down bullets and shells. At first the shells went very wide for their fire was bad but after a time they got our range and then they fairly mopped us. I saw shells bursting right and left of me and I saw many a good comrade go out.[30]

An artillery officer noted tersely, 'West Kents, Middlesex and Northumberlands decimated by shell fire.'

Sergeant John Collins, serving with the Royal Army Medical Corps attached to 7 Brigade, also experienced the effects of this shelling, recalling: 'I heard the shell bursts above my head, a shrapnel shell, highish burst, white smoke and the bullets came down whistling like all the hobs of hell, as if a thousand whistles had been turned on.'[31] Sergeant Ernest White of 18 Hussars had a not dissimilar experience:

> I myself was sent on a patrol to a canal. It was very confused. We had a number of South African campaigners [almost certainly Reservists] and they couldn't understand it, they had never seen anything like it because you were under shell fire most of the time. They were very heavy with machine guns and artillery.[32]

Tom Bridges and his soldiers from C Squadron, 4 Dragoon Guards had also been in the thick of it. In fact, it was a soldier from C Squadron who fired the first British shot of the war on the day before the fighting started in earnest at Mons. At dawn on 22 August C Squadron had pushed out two officers' patrols from Obourg, just north of the canal at Mons, towards Soignies. One of these encountered a German piquet on the road, opened fire on it and drove it off:

> We had just finished watering our horses at a crossroads when the first Uhlan scouts were sighted, four men riding down the main road. We were hidden from view and I dismounted two troops for fire action and kept two mounted ready to charge. But 300 yards away the Uhlans saw something suspicious, halted and turned back along the road. In answer to his urgent entreaty I loosed Hornby with two troops down the road after them and mounting the rest followed at a trot ... The chase went merrily down the hard high road for about a mile and a half. We caught them at the village of Soignies where there was a regular melee. The Uhlans were hampered by their long lances and a good many threw them away. Several were killed, Hornby for one running his man through.[33]

Although the resistance put up by II Corps that day was truly remarkable, the decision to withdraw was, without doubt, the only rational option for Sir John French. The initial withdrawal from Mons marked the beginning of a retreat that would last a fortnight and take the BEF back over 170 miles, almost to the gates of Paris.

Of course, General Haldane and the men under his command in 10 Brigade would have been largely unaware of the drama that was unfolding at Mons. Almost as soon as the men of 10 Brigade arrived at Le Cateau, they were on the march. The Royal Dublin Fusiliers and the Royal Warwickshires, together with the rest of the brigade, set off along the main road from Le Cateau to Cambrai at 10.30am on the morning of 24 August to take up their initial positions around the village of Beaumont, 5 miles to the north-west of Le Cateau.

Captain Hart of the Royal Warwickshires described the battalion's first proper march of the war:

> It was a stiff climb, uphill all the way. The day was very hot without any shade from the poplars along the roadside. The

men found it very trying. It was necessary to give stringent orders with regard to water and to prevent the men giving their water bottles to the willing and well-meaning small boys to take away to fill.[34]

Private Hill, also with the Warwickshires, recounted the day's events in similar terms:

We marched out of the town along a typical French road. Just when we were about all in, a halt was called for dinner, which we never had as an outburst of artillery fire was heard. It must have been miles away but we had orders to open out to artillery formation and proceed. We saw no enemy that day and at night bivouacked in a cornfield where we enjoyed a long delayed dinner.[35]

The men were in fact marching along the very road that would be at the centre of the battle at Le Cateau two days later.

Haldane set up his brigade headquarters in the village brewery. Outposts were established to the north-east of the town, the most likely direction from which enemy forces might be expected to arrive. The Dublin Fusiliers arrived at Inchy ahead of the Warwickshires and both battalions pitched camp together near the village and tried to grab as much rest as possible. They had been on the move for the best part of 48 hours.

Corporal O'Donnell of the Royal Dublin Fusiliers recalled the scene at the camp site about half a mile from the church at Inchy:

We had tea about 5pm, everyone quite happy and satisfied. Just as we had finished, the [Seaforth Highlanders and Royal Warwickshires] swung into the same field. Everything was quiet and silent. The village butcher doled out beer free to all and all the villagers congregated around, while one woman near the hedge was shaving in a most expert manner as many men as she could manage – others brought water for washing. We were near an orchard and the lady proprietor handed it over to the Brigade which was much appreciated.[36]

Later that evening O'Donnell and the rest of D Company mounted outposts about 2 miles to the front of the brigade positions. They stopped vehicles and pedestrians alike, checking for spies and Germans. O'Donnell was a fluent French speaker, and before the war he had taught languages at St Enda's College in Dublin: 'I had to teach the men how to halt the people. It took 20 minutes. "Halte la!" "Levez les mains!" It was rather amusing.'

Mainwaring himself, in a statement he prepared after the court martial, claimed that he got no sleep on 24 August, as, in his own words, 'I had to see that everything and everybody was ready to move.'[37] In truth, Mainwaring was not in good health. Prior to the outbreak of the war he had been subject to periods of illness that required him to take to his bed. In September 1913, while his battalion was on manoeuvres, he suffered a bad fit of colitis and had to return to Gravesend to recover. Haldane was of the opinion that Mainwaring was not fit for active service. When war was declared he tried to get him 'spun', or relieved of his command, on medical grounds but 'did not succeed as the doctors did not support me'.[38] The conditions under which Mainwaring was now forced to operate must have tested his physical reserves to the absolute limit.

Mainwaring's health was not Haldane's only concern. It was obvious that Haldane had a low opinion of Mainwaring as a soldier and commanding officer. The diary he kept at Shorncliffe, now in the Imperial War Museum, is full of uncomplimentary references to him and other officers of the Royal Dublin Fusiliers. For example, in his diary entry for 26 August 1913, a year to the day before the battle at Le Cateau, Haldane described some of the officers of the battalion as 'very stupid at grasping an order no matter how clearly and carefully given'.[39] It is not clear whether this was a direct reference to Mainwaring, but there is more than a hint that it was. The kindest reference to Mainwaring is that he 'commanded in defence satisfactorily', but even this is hardly a ringing endorsement.

It is not clear whether Elkington got any rest on the 24th either. In a statement he prepared for the court martial in September, he made no reference to 24 August at all, but it is highly unlikely that he would have done so. As a diligent and committed professional soldier, he would have been just as busy and involved in the movements of his battalion as Mainwaring had been. In Elkington's case, however, all the evidence suggests that his overall health was good and that he had a much more robust constitution than Mainwaring.

Haldane also had a much higher opinion of Elkington than he did of Mainwaring. On 4 September 1913 Haldane's diary records his view that 'Elkington leads his battalion well.' Later, in the spring of 1914, as the brigade was preparing for participation in divisional exercises, Haldane noted that 'Elkington has written the best orders.'[40]

Elkington, along with all of the commanding officers of the battalions involved, was operating under a steadily increasing pressure. This was also true of the brigade commander himself. Haldane had certainly not slept since the brigade had started on its journey to France and would not do so for several days yet.

The battalion commander with whom it seems Haldane had the strongest and most positive relationship was Sir Evelyn Bradford, who commanded the Seaforth Highlanders. Bradford had taken command of the Seaforths in June 1913 and had brought about a marked change in discipline, including stamping down hard on the culture of drunkenness that had seriously impaired the efficiency of the battalion. Unfortunately Bradford was killed leading his battalion forward during the advance to the Aisne in the first few days of September. His death was a huge personal blow to Haldane, who had come to rely heavily on his advice and counsel since the brigade had landed in France.

Haldane's particular *bête noire* was Colonel Churcher, who commanded the remaining battalion in the brigade, the 1st Royal Irish Fusiliers, and had done so since the autumn of 1910. Haldane thought he was a total dud. In his diary he described Churcher as a 'humbug' who was only interested in sport and could not be relied upon to bring about any improvement in his battalion whatsoever. In a decisive act of leadership, Haldane had him sent back to England during the retreat from Mons. Haldane described Churcher's behaviour as 'so unsatisfactory' that he had to be relieved of his command.[41] Judging by the highly personal nature of his comments about Churcher in his pre-war diary, Haldane must have taken particular pleasure in this action. It is not clear what Churcher did to earn this ignominy. There is nothing in the war diaries of the battalion or brigade, nor in any of Haldane's subsequent writing, that refers to any incidents involving Churcher's actions. Churcher, however, unlike Elkington and Mainwaring, did not face a court martial. In his case, the army chose not to wash its dirty laundry in public, and the nature of his misdemeanour remains hidden from history. The behaviour of Elkington and Mainwaring, by contrast, would attract the full glare of publicity.

To the north of 10 Brigade's new positions at Beaumont, II Corps, having inflicted severe damage on the Germans at Mons, had successfully disengaged from the enemy and moved back in accordance with GHQ's instructions to a new line around the villages of Bavai, St Waast, Bermeries, Wargnies, Jenlain and Saultain, some 17 miles or so from 10 Brigade at Beaumont. (This explains why 10 Brigade saw nothing of either II Corps or the enemy on 24 August.) The immediate retreat from Mons during the evening of 23 August to these new positions 2 to 3 miles south of the canal had been conducted without any great problems. The enemy had taken a hard knock during the course of the first day's fighting at Mons and was in no great hurry to chase the retiring British forces that night. To the amazement of the British troops at Mons, German bugles were even heard to sound the 'cease fire' all along the front line as it began to turn dark, almost as if they were on field manoeuvres. After some singing at one place it all went quiet for the night. The enemy in fact even displayed some nervousness that the British would launch a night attack and illuminating flares were fired throughout the night – the first time British soldiers had seen such devices.

But as dawn broke on 24 August vicious fighting erupted again all along the new line held by II Corps. The Germans were pushing forward hard and fast on both the right and left flanks of Smith-Dorrien's force as they continued to complete their outflanking movements. Massed infantry attacks were launched against the British positions, with very much the same consequences as the day before. Alf Tebbutt, a private soldier serving in the 1st Lincolns of 9 Brigade, 3 Division recorded: 'I just kept firing away at the mass of Germans in front of me until my rifle was too hot to hold. At 400 yards you couldn't miss and I never thought to see so many dead and wounded men in such a small space.'[42]

Although their comrades-in-arms were invisible to them, the sounds of gunfire must have been audible to Elkington, Mainwaring and their men. A lively resistance had been put up all day by II Corps, slowing the German advance and restricting it to a meagre 3 or 4 miles. Meanwhile 5 Division, together with the help of cavalry units and the infantry of 19 Brigade, had parried von Kluck's attempt to encircle the retreating

British forces. During the day an extraordinary action had been fought at Elouges, where the entire German *IV Corps*, consisting of *7* and *8 Divisions* and supported by nine artillery batteries, was launched against two British battalions of 13 Brigade, units of two cavalry brigades and two batteries of guns. Astonishingly, the two battalions, the 1st Norfolks and 1st Cheshires, were able to inflict heavy losses upon their attackers. Tom Lawrence, serving with the Norfolks, recalled: 'We were on a little ridge, Cheshires on our left, 119 Battery on our right and a clear field of fire across cornfields to the north-west. Might have been back home in Norfolk! We hadn't any time to dig in and so were sitting ducks for their gunners, but they weren't much good.'[43]

L Battery of VII Brigade, Royal Horse Artillery came into action at about 1pm, just to the west of Elouges. Firing low-burst shrapnel at the German infantry advancing from Quievrain at 2,000 yards' range, they simply 'mowed down the advancing masses'.[44] German attempts to silence the guns of L battery failed and their infantry remained tied up in the village, unable to move forward. The position was not, however, sustainable and at around 4pm the British guns were pulled back and the Norfolks and Cheshires were ordered to withdraw. The Norfolks managed to pull out but the Cheshires never received their orders to retire. So they stayed, fought and died in their hundreds. The battalion had begun the day more than a thousand strong, but only 200 of them made it back to the British lines. A German survivor of the action at Elouges later recalled: 'They fired like devils. Simply to move was to invite destruction. In our first attack we lost nearly a whole battalion.'

Tom Bridges was heavily involved in the action at Elouges, although on this occasion his contribution was short-lived and not very effective:

At noon 2 Cavalry Brigade was quietly watering in the village of Andregnies. Our reconnaissance must have been at fault for the German infantry was at that very moment steadily advancing on this village and almost within rifle shot of it. I debouched at the head of my squadron from the northern entrance of the village at a gallop, drawing swords as we went and dashing up a lane between wire fences on to a rise where there was a solitary cottage which seemed like a likely point d'appui. But as we topped the rise we came under heavy rifle fire and my horse fell down on his nose with a broken leg and most of the squadron and machine gun section seemed to gallop over me and I received a heavy blow to my face. I saw them swinging off to the right and then lost consciousness for a time.[45]

Bridges regained consciousness inside the cottage, which held some Red Cross orderlies and wounded soldiers. What he saw from the cottage shook him:

> I could scarcely believe my eyes. Marching through the corn in open order and perfect formation, with fixed bayonets glinting in the sun, were line upon line of grey-green German infantry. The nearest could not have been more than 200 yards away. This sight galvanized me into action and the back door being barricaded, I went through the open window like the clown in a pantomime. I crawled [on to the back of a nearby horse] and we ambled off in the direction of the village, sole target it seemed for a whole German army corps until we reached dead ground and the cover of houses.[46]

It seems that Bridges, having escaped through the back of the cottage, found a horse and made good his escape, beginning a search for his regiment that would take two days and involve several narrow escapes.

But the cost of all this bravery and heroic defence had been very high. On 24 August II Corps sustained even higher casualties than it had at Mons the day before. A further 2,200 men were dead, wounded or missing by nightfall. The physical strains of the last few hectic days were by now beginning to show:

> Long after nightfall the battalions of 3 Division were passing the crossroads in Bavai, the men stumbling along more like ghosts than living soldiers, unconscious of everything about them, but still moving under the magic impulse of discipline and regimental pride. Marching they were hardly awake; halted, whether sitting or standing, they were instantly asleep. And this, it must be borne in mind, was only the beginning of the retreat.[47]

Major Geiger of the 2nd Royal Welch Fusiliers, part of 19 Brigade, recounted the growing sense of concern over events on 24 August:

> We halted at midday in a field near Rombies where we started to dig in with our entrenching tools. We had hardly scratched the soil and eaten some bully beef and biscuit when we moved off again. The day was very hot. Before long we began to see signs that a retreat was in progress: packs which had been cast off were lying by the roadside. In spite of the heat the men had marched well but it was becoming apparent that the Reservists' boots were going to give trouble. During the march and on later marches wine was offered to the men so liberally that a check had to be kept on its consumption, sometimes by breaking the bottles.[48]

As II Corps continued its retreat the next day, heading southwards towards Le Cateau itself, so Elkington, Mainwaring and the men they commanded were hurrying in the opposite direction, straight into the path of the German forces, to provide a rearguard for Smith-Dorrien's retiring force, in accordance with the directions Snow had received from Henry Wilson.

Late in the evening of 24 August 10 Brigade had received orders from GHQ to move northwards directly into the enemy's path. Its task was to provide the rearguard for the rest of II Corps. At 2am Elkington and Mainwaring led their men on another route march, this time of 8 miles, to a position just to the south-west of St Python, a small village on the northern outskirts of Solesmes. The two battalions arrived 4 hours later, and promptly set about preparing breakfast. It would be their only meal of the day. An hour later gunfire became audible from the north-east as fighting erupted again between the retiring II Corps and the advancing Germans. The enemy forces were closing in.

For Private Hill it was another gruelling morning: 'We marched off in columns of fours next morning in a new direction ... we halted, piled arms and rations were issued – the last for many days. Men were told off to dig trenches on rising ground to our left.'[49]

When the Royal Warwickshires and the Royal Dublin Fusiliers arrived at Solesmes in the early hours of 25 August, they took up initial positions behind the railway embankment about a mile to the south of the village.

Elkington and Mainwaring both had doubts about this new position, as did Haldane, as the ground did not provide a good enough field of fire. The battalions duly fell back to the higher ground to the rear. Here the men were set to work digging their first trenches of the war. For most of the rest of the morning things were fairly quiet. There was no sign of the enemy and little sign of II Corps either.

What was on display that morning was some evidence of the men's naivety about the type of warfare they were engaged in. General Snow had ordered 12 Brigade to extend its lines further to the west, and went to see how they were getting on:

> I was horrified when I went to visit them to find that they had piled arms in an open space on a slope facing the direction of the enemy and had taken off their accoutrements and hung them up on the piles of rifles. Had artillery fire been opened there would have been a disaster. I was very angry and such a thing never happened again ...[50]

Solesmes needed to be strongly defended because all the roads from the north-east, north and north-west converged upon it, and these were the roads being used by II Corps in its attempt to continue its escape to the south. If the roads were not kept open, the British forces would face encirclement and almost certain defeat at the hands of the enemy. To all intents and purposes, British involvement in the war would be over.

The division was about to be reinforced by its artillery. As dawn broke on the 25th a train carrying XXXVII (Howitzer) Brigade was de-training at Fresnoy le Grand, some 15 miles to the south. The batteries were ordered to move off immediately and the eager gunners were ready to come into action at short notice. Captain Pusey, however, could sense that the overall situation was not good: 'It was not long, however, before we were aware that all was not well. Large columns of transport continued to pass the Battery in the opposite direction and we wondered why. We were soon to learn ...'.[51]

Soon after midday a large mass of British transport vehicles attempted to pass through Solesmes along roads that were already crowded with refugees fleeing from the advancing German forces. It was a scene of noise and confusion. The sense of things beginning to go seriously wrong with the British campaign must have been obvious to Elkington's and Mainwaring's men. Captain Hart recalled:

> During the early part of the afternoon, not only was the sound of guns closer but the burst of shells could be seen not many miles away on our left front, and as the afternoon wore on, the tide of battle could be seen slowly but surely creeping towards us. We were, however, still wrapped in the fog of war and I have no recollection at any time of the day of hearing the slightest sound or noise indicative of battle towards our right in the direction of the retirement of II Corps.[52]

At around 4pm both the battalions moved further east to new positions to the north of Fontaine au Tertre farm and again began to dig in. At about 5.30pm, just as it began to rain steadily, both battalions came under direct shell fire for the first time. German artillery from the north-east had opened up a sporadic bombardment of their positions, but there were no reported casualties. The artillery attached to 4 Division did not return fire, as the gun crews could not locate the positions of the German guns.

Lieutenant Macky of the Royal Dublin Fusiliers would later describe these moments at Solesmes:

> My company took up the foremost position and dug lying cover as only entrenching tools were available. The Somerset Light Infantry were on our right and the Seaforth Highlanders in support. We faced due north. We could hear heavy fighting in the distance. We had an excellent field of fire and were told to expect enemy cavalry. In the afternoon rain fell heavily and we then came for the first time under enemy shell fire, the Somersets getting the worst of it, being near a clump of trees which offered a good ranging mark for the enemy artillery. No shell actually struck the line of the battalion which was lucky as we had no cover from artillery fire.[53]

Somewhat unfairly, given the tools that were to hand, Snow was contemptuous of these early efforts to entrench: 'In spite of what the troops had learned in the Boer War, in spite of what they had been taught, all they had done was to make a few scratchings of the nature of what was called 50 years ago a shelter pit, of no use whatever against any sort of fire.'[54]

Private Hill remembered how the shelling began:

> an aeroplane hovered over us. It had no distinguishing marks and we thought it was French, but were soon disillusioned as it scattered coloured lights over us. Too late, we opened fire. Soon large black shells were bursting in the beet field just in front of our improvised position. Rain then started, the shelling ceased and a regiment of our cavalry came galloping up and jumped over us in our hastily constructed trench.[55]

At about the same time 19 Brigade, an independent unit attached to II Corps and made up of Lines of Communication troops, began to pass through the positions held by 10 Brigade at St Python on its way south, passing up the Selle valley by way of Briastre and Neuvilly to Le Cateau. A brigade of cavalry also began passing through St Python, falling back towards Viesly and the south-west. Captain James Jack of the 1st Cameronians recalled the conditions of the march on that blisteringly hot day: 'The men are becoming tired and footsore. The incessant blocks on the congested roads make straggling difficult to prevent.'[56]

One of the battalions attached to 19 Brigade was the 2nd Royal Welch Fusiliers. Captain Dunn, the battalion's medical officer, recounted some of their movements:

> As we were marching through St Python word was passed that the enemy was near and shortly after we cleared the village a few shells fell in it. We could see the enemy in the distance advancing in artillery formation. They started to shell the ground on our right. The first shell burst about 400 yards from us, near a troop of our cavalry, who soon moved out of sight. Shells then burst nearer to where we were. Suddenly there was a bang and a noise like tearing calico as a couple of shells in close succession burst over us. This was the first time we had been under fire and since no one was hit the men began to make merry with one another on the subject.[57]

Lieutenant Robert Money, serving with the 1st Cameronians in 19 Brigade, described his unit's retreat through Solesmes:

> Cavalry, wagons, guns all over the place; it was a rather narrow village street. We thought we were going to see some action at last – we were rather excited. Over the crest, about 15,000 yards away, we saw something moving and we put our Barr & Stroud [telescopic range finder] on it and saw it was three enormous columns of Germans moving across this open country in mass formation and it really was like the whole hillside was moving. The nearest they came was about 10,000 yards which was very much out of range as far as we were concerned.[58]

Captain Jack had similar memories of Solesmes on this day, remarking: 'Solesmes [was] crammed with the transport of our cavalry moving east, with French cavalry going west, with units of our 3 Division and a stream of refugees and wagons clearing off southwards. An awful mix up ...'.[59]

Lieutenant Henry Barton Owens, a young surgeon serving with 3 Cavalry Field Ambulance, was also passing through the town at this time, and described how, 'We stopped in Solesmes for several hours, waiting. Several infantry regiments, the Argyll and Sutherland Highlanders and the Manchesters, came through. We moved off from Solesmes about 5pm in a deuce of a crush of transport, guns and ammunition columns.'[60]

By 8pm it was evident that British troops had now cleared Solesmes and were well on the way south towards their new defensive lines at Le Cateau, while 4 Division had been ordered to hold its ground at Solesmes to cover the retirement of 3 Division, 19 Brigade and the cavalry. Their job being done, both battalions began their own moves southwards. The Royal Warwickshires moved off at 10pm, with the Royal Dublin Fusiliers following an hour later. Before marching away from St Python, Mainwaring's men had spotted German Uhlans in front of the farm and opened fire on them, hitting some of the enemy cavalry. It was their first engagement of the war.

Corporal O'Donnell heard these first shots fired in anger by his comrades:

About 11pm there was a sudden burst of rifle fire from the men in the orchard – the first shots fired by the Dublins in the War. It lasted about two minutes. We in the farmyard [at Fontaine au Tertre Farm] could hear the footbeat of the enemy's cavalry for miles racing back along the road. A little later, a riderless horse belonging to the Germans was led in by one of our men.[61]

A short while later the Seaforths also fired on some approaching German cavalry.

Haldane felt that the deployment to St Python had been good for morale:

Towards evening the German cavalry put in an appearance but were driven off each time they came near us with the loss of some men and horses. The men enjoyed lying in wait for them on either side of the road, with a rope stretched across it and this brush with the enemy had the effect of raising their morale.[62]

Snow, in contrast, would later express the view that the division's deployment to Solesmes was a 'waste of force':

Whether we were much more than moral support I am not sure. We certainly should have prevented any turning movement from the north-west but whether any German troops were near enough to try such a movement I doubt. It was very unlikely that such a movement could have been attempted by any other than cavalry and this could have been secured against by employing one of my brigades, leaving two brigades free to continue the preparation of the Le Cateau position. We may have accomplished our purpose but it was a waste of force. 4 Division was supposed to have done a great deal of good by their intervention and was supposed to have been well handled. As a matter of fact there was very little intervention and still less handling. Our losses for the day were trivial.[63]

Some of the troops heading south from Solesmes during 25 August travelled over the gentle slopes of the shallow valley of the River Selle.

Major Geiger described the conditions that faced the exhausted men that evening:

> Towards dusk we were all pretty leg-weary in spite of the frequent halts we made. The men had been without sleep for a couple of nights so it was difficult to keep them going. As we passed guns on the road we saw drivers asleep on their horses' backs. Belfield, our Armourer-Sergeant, told how during one of the halts of the transport he waited so long for the wagons to move on that he walked up the line to see what was the reason for the stoppage, and found the driver of the leading wagon asleep.[64]

Captain Jack of the Cameronians was also marching his men up the Selle Valley at about the same time:

> Rain is falling heavily as I trot up the attractive valley of the Selle. On the slopes just south of Neuvilly and Montay, the 4 Division, fresh from England, is digging trenches. It gives one a feeling of security to pass back through infantry in position. I devoutly hope that other fresh divisions from the same source are at hand.[65]

Lieutenant Owens also saw the same reassuring sights:

> It was a cold, dark evening, raining steadily. Saw shrapnel bursting behind Solesmes. Passed through lines of our infantry lying in readiness in shallow scraped trenches on both sides of the road. Some had packs and greatcoats. Some had ground sheets. They looked very wet and cold. Some of our guns on hills to the right were firing.[66]

Jack was, however, misguided in his hopes that other troops were ready to reinforce the BEF, as the men of 4 Division were the only effective protection II Corps now had against the advancing German Army. The last remaining division in England was the 6th, and it would not be sent to France until the middle of September.

Earlier in the day 5 Division had begun its move southwards from Bavai. Corporal Fred Atkinson of the 1st Battalion, Royal West Kents, part of that division's 13 Brigade, recounted his memories of the retreat to Le Cateau:

> Of course we had to make a detour you see, we couldn't go as the crow flies and that is what caused the very long and difficult marches. The sun was hot and blazing and dusty roads nearly choked us. There were men with bleeding feet and their tongues rattled in their mouth like a piece of wood against their teeth for want of a drink of water. If ever anyone valued a drop of water it was then.[67]

During the course of the afternoon 4 Division had been ordered, as soon as it was prudently possible, to take up a position the following day on the left flank of II Corps at Le Cateau. From there, the plan was for the division to retreat southwards. At 6.40pm Divisional HQ received instructions from GHQ to hold a 3-mile front stretching from Fontaine au Pire to Wambaix; 11 and 12 Brigades were to hold the front line, with 10 Brigade in reserve at Haucourt. This new order would take the division towards the south-west, directly into the path of the right flank of the advancing German armies. Thus 4 Division would in effect be taking up a position on the extreme left of the BEF, protecting its flank.

Up until this point it seems clear, both from the Brigade War Diary and from the testimony of Mainwaring in particular, that Haldane was in regular contact with his battalion commanders. On 24 August Mainwaring records being told by Haldane that the battalion would be marching north to cover the retirement of the BEF. The following day Haldane sent for Mainwaring and informed him that the brigade had to remain where it was at Solesmes until the whole of the British forces in front of them had passed through. But even though he was in communication with his battalion commanders, Haldane was keeping the flow of information to a minimum: 'I had become aware that all was not going well ... I kept silence so far as everyone in my Brigade was concerned, as the last thing I wished to do was to damp the high spirits of the officers and men.'[68]

However regular the contact had been between Haldane and the others, the retirement from Solesmes marked the beginning of a period of total breakdown in communications between Haldane, Elkington and Mainwaring. Mainwaring claimed that after the march from Solesmes began on the evening of 25 August he never saw Haldane again, nor did he receive any order of any sort from him. The same was true for Elkington. This breakdown in communication is also confirmed by Haldane himself, in an account compiled a fortnight later. On 9 September Haldane wrote an account for General Snow of the actions he took on 26 August while commanding the brigade during the fighting at Le Cateau. It began with a curious apology: 'I regret that the whole of the orders and messages received and sent by me that day were lost with my Staff Officer's horse. I can therefore only speak from recollection.'[69] He then went on to make a startling admission about what happened during the night march from Solesmes to Haucourt:

> My infantry, which was preceded by the first line transport, in front of which I was marching with the Divisional Commander, became detached from me and when I reported myself to the 4 Division Commander I had not ascertained where it was. I at once accompanied the Divisional Commander on his personal reconnaissance of the position [at Haucourt]. Before this was completed, the Germans had begun the attack and my Brigade, as I afterwards ascertained, dispersed to occupy the best position in its vicinity.[70]

Haldane did manage to link up during the course of the early morning of 26 August with two of his battalions, the Royal Irish and the Seaforth Highlanders, but no communication at all could be established with the Royal Warwickshires and the Royal Dublin Fusiliers, as a direct consequence of the difficulties encountered during the night march from Solesmes.

Haldane probably became detached from a large part of his brigade at Beauvois, where it was necessary for some reason to reverse the direction of march in the middle of the village. The village was crowded with troops and transports and the change in direction took considerable time and effort to organise. With the first line transport at the front of the march, gaps clearly opened up in the column of infantry. At some point along the way Haldane seems also to have taken a wrong turn and ended up in Cattenieres. It was here that he first discovered he had become separated from the bulk of his brigade:

> I was horrified, though not exactly surprised, when riding back a short way at daylight to find no signs of the infantry. I had ordered the horses to be watered, wood to be collected, fires lighted and kettles boiled soon after reaching Cattenieres as I knew that the infantry when they came up would be exhausted by their tedious tramp and hoped to have tea ready for them. But no signs of troops were visible and a cyclist orderly who had ridden back for some distance along our tracks returned with the report that nothing was coming along the road behind us.[71]

Haldane would find it impossible to re-establish contact once the fighting at Le Cateau started soon after 6am on 26 August. Almost as soon as the brigade had reached its destination, the German forces began their attack. Haldane, Elkington and Mainwaring were all immediately thrown in at the deep end of an intense firefight, not knowing each other's whereabouts. Thus Haldane's ability to command the brigade effectively during the next few critical hours would be seriously undermined.

General Snow would also later express his own remorse for the haphazard way in which the division retired from St Python to its new positions around Haucourt during the evening and early morning of 25/26 August. In a typically self-critical account, he remarked:

> I have often wondered since how I could have left the troops and ridden on to Haucourt in such a careless frame of mind. Although I quite realised we might have to fight on the morrow, I knew the troops were practically on the position assigned to them and that the Brigadiers would see that the positions were taken up as soon as it was light enough to see what they were about and I knew the troops were covered by outposts. What I did not realise, and I ought to have known, was that the Germans were so close on my heels; another instance of want of imagination.[72]

Haucourt itself was a small, inconspicuous village 10 miles to the south-east of Cambrai. Some 800 yards in front of the village lay the gently rising banks of the Warnelle Ravine, a natural defensive screen but one that also impeded visibility over the approaches to 10 Brigade's new positions. The men had marched a distance of 12 miles in the pouring rain. Their route had taken them through the villages of Quiévy, Bevillers and Beauvois. The darkness was punctuated only by the dark red glow of villages set on fire by German shelling towards the northern horizon.

Captain Hart of the Royal Warwickshires could not later recall the exact route the battalion took, but the evidence of conflict and destruction left an enduring impression on him:

> It seemed as if we were continually winding along to our right [westward]; and in the earlier part of the night wherever we went or turned we kept seeing a burning village ahead of us and every time we saw it again it looked closer than when we had last seen it. We got to hate the sight of it.[73]

General Snow described the night as 'very dark and the whole sky to the northward was lit up by what we thought were burning villages. As a matter of fact they were probably only big fires lighted to dry the men's clothes by after the soaking rain.'[74] It seems, however, highly unlikely that the men would have stopped to light fires, given their rising levels of exhaustion and the urgency of getting to their new positions. Haldane also recalled 'the inky dark, though it is true that to our rear the lurid glare of burning farms and haystacks shed a fitful light upon the scene'.[75]

Captain Clarke of the Royal Dublin Fusiliers provided a good account of the conditions of this night march the following year in a magazine article:

> It was a most trying march. Men had been on the move since 2am the previous day. There had been little time for rest or food as they were always on the qui vive, entrenching, getting soaked by the rain, shelled in the farm and attacked by night. Several of the reservists also had come from some quiet employment which did not tend to harden the feet or keep them fit to carry the heavy marching order kit they had worn all that hot August day.

So the conditions for a night march were hardly ideal. Men did their level best (they always do that), but they fell asleep as they marched and dropped from sheer exhaustion.

I know that I, at times, staggered across the road trying to keep awake. I had had no sleep the night before nor the night we landed and was very weary.[76]

The march also left a profound impression on Private Hill of the Royal Warwickshires: 'That night we seemed to march round and round a burning farmhouse. Day broke and we were still dragging our weary limbs along in what seemed to us an everlasting circle. At last the word came to halt and fall out for a couple of hours' rest.' Likewise, for Lieutenant Macky, the march would be remembered for the scenes of destruction that were now all too obvious: 'The brigade marched off [from Fontaine au Tertre] as quietly as possible towards Caudry. Villages were burning in front of and on each side of us.'[77]

The march took the best part of 6 hours to complete, but both battalions began to arrive on the eastern outskirts of the village at about 5am, much later than had been planned. Some of the delay was due to the fact that 3 Division was heavily engaged throughout the day in a running fight with the Germans. As a result, it was late in the day – well after 10pm – before 4 Division was able to relinquish the ground it held as rearguard to II Corps. The movements of the division were also delayed by the march across their line of retirement of Sordet's Cavalry Corps, which was taking up positions around Walincourt.

The Royal Warwickshires immediately bivouacked in a cornfield by the side of the road from Ligny. The Royal Dublin Fusiliers were just behind Elkington's men on the same road. The exhausted soldiers of both battalions began taking off their equipment, desperate for some rest before they resumed their march south. Many of them collapsed on the spot. Iron rations – emergency reserves of food – were issued. As they ate their bully beef and biscuits, the men snatched what rest they could along that quiet, peaceful country lane. Few of them can have had any understanding of the events of the previous 48 hours, and why they were retreating in the first place. Surely none could have imagined the disaster that was about to unfold around them. Unfortunately, the same was true of their senior officers, including Elkington and Mainwaring. Even

General Snow confessed to having little knowledge of what was going on around him: 'Since the night before [24 August] I had had no information of any sort from anyone.'[78]

Among the more senior army commanders there was a growing realisation of the danger facing the BEF, even if Snow himself remained oblivious to it. The British troops had come up against vastly superior forces that were executing, skilfully and methodically and without regard to their own casualties, a very carefully designed plan to encircle and overwhelm both the British and French forces operating on the left of the Allied front. The strength of this encircling movement was also becoming clearer to French and his corps commanders, as were the growing gaps in the Allied lines. But it was far from clear where and how the Germans would strike next. GHQ was not even sure where the main bulk of the German Army was located. It was in fact much closer to II Corps than anyone thought.

Oblivious to most of these strategic considerations, Mainwaring himself concentrated on the immediate situation he now faced as his men tried to rest after the exhausting night march. He sent his adjutant to seek orders from Haldane about what the Royal Dublin Fusiliers were to do next. But there was no sign of either the brigade commander or any of his staff. Haldane was out with Snow inspecting the ground ahead and could not be contacted by any of his battalion commanders. Perhaps more importantly, at least as far as the troops were concerned, there was no sign of the hot tea envisaged by Haldane's thoughtful action at Cattenieres. Mainwaring had, however, been told by one of General Snow's staff officers, Colonel Edmonds, that the march would resume at 7am for another 12 miles or so en route to Le Catelet. One can only imagine Mainwaring's reaction to this news. Over the course of the last two days the officers and men of both battalions had already marched 25 miles in extremely difficult conditions, with little food or rest.

As would soon become clear, the Germans were close on the heels of the retreating British forces. Uhlans had been spotted at Solesmes by the Royal Dublin Fusiliers an hour or so before Elkington and Mainwaring began their own withdrawal, although these were the only enemy soldiers seen so far by any of the men in Elkington's and Mainwaring's battalions. But all this was to change in the course of the next few hours at Haucourt as the first shots were fired in the fighting at Le Cateau.

The lack of the division's 'eyes and ears', which arose because of the way the division had been deployed to France, would soon bring disastrous consequences. The divisional cavalry (a squadron of 19 Hussars) and cyclists had been left behind, and the division had no heavy artillery battery, no field engineers, no signallers and no medical support teams at all. The men had moved through the night with no mounted troops to provide a protective screen or to establish the whereabouts of enemy forces. There were no 60-pounders to mow down enemy infantry as they prepared to attack, no engineers to prepare defensive positions and supervise working parties. They could not have been more unprepared for what was about to befall them. II Corps would also have to face the enemy on its own, with its right and left flanks open and unprotected. In order to effect the most rapid retreat, Sir John French had split up the BEF on 25 August, pushing the two corps down separate escape routes.

The route of the BEF's retirement towards Le Cateau on 25 August had presented French and GHQ with a serious logistical problem. The large bulk of retreating British and French soldiers, joined by a clogging mass of civilian refugees, meant that the roads towards the south-west were in danger of jamming up. The retreat was in danger of being seriously compromised by the congestion, and French knew that any delay could have catastrophic consequences, especially if the Germans caught up with the retreating British forces and engaged them while they were in no position to properly defend themselves.

Immediately to the south of Bavai, which marked the junction between I and II Corps, lay the Forest of Mormal, a thick block of woodland some 9 miles long by 4 miles wide. There was a good, straight road running along the western edge of the forest, but if the whole of the BEF were to try to pass along it to Le Cateau, it would mean a flank march across the front of the advancing Germans who were already threatening the British left flank. Passing entirely along the eastern side of the forest was equally problematic because of the large numbers of French troops in the vicinity and the consequent risk of traffic jams developing. Faced with this difficult choice, French took the calculated risk to divide his forces. Thus I Corps was sent east and II Corps west of the forest, and orders to this effect were sent by GHQ at 8.25pm on the evening of 25 August. French had it in his mind that both corps would take up a position centred on Le Cateau and form a continuous front facing the Germans.

Lord Edward Gleichen, commanding 15 Brigade of 5 Division, marched with his men down the western side of the forest on 25 August:

> It seemed a very long march that day, down the perfectly straight road skirting the Mormal Forest and on to Le Cateau. It was, as a matter of fact, only a little over twenty miles but the hot day, with very little food, was most trying for the men. We had one good rest at Englefontaine where we bought a lot of food – bread, cheese, apples and plums and a little meat – but it was not much. The rest of the road was bare and hot, leading over down-like country past the town of Le Cateau and on to the heights to the west of it. Many aeroplanes, British, French and German, were skimming about and numerous bodies of French cavalry could be seen moving about the downs and the roads in the rear.[79]

As events would turn out, it would be a hair-raising 8 days before the two halves of the British Army would be reunited. For Elkington and Mainwaring and all those in II Corps, the decision to split the BEF in this way would be perhaps the definitive factor that determined the shape of the battle that would begin the following morning.

Chapter 3

26 August: Crisis at Le Cateau

We're here because we're here
Because we're here because we're here;
We're here because we're here
Because we're here, because we're here.

from a popular song

Sir John French's plans for 26 August were simple and straightforward enough.[80] The BEF would continue its withdrawal to the south, avoid contact with the enemy wherever possible, and try to keep in touch with the French forces on its flanks, thus preventing an encirclement of the BEF and so avoiding a disastrous defeat. I and II Corps would meet up at Le Cateau during the night of the 25th and retire in good order in the early hours of the following morning. Sir John French naturally and correctly wanted both corps of his army to stay together so they could provide mutual support. On 26 August, however, nothing would go according to plan.

While II Corps began arriving in dribs and drabs at Le Cateau during 25 August, I Corps had already come to a halt 8 miles away at Landrecies to the south-east. Haig would make no further attempt to establish contact with the other half of the BEF that night. Both 1 and 2 Divisions had made excellent progress in making good their escape during the day and had successfully avoided serious contact with the enemy, although a number of rearguard actions – some quite heavy – were fought during the morning and afternoon.

Walter Burchmore served with the Royal Horse Artillery that day, protecting the retreat of I Corps. He recalled:

Fighting on the way back to Landrecies, good gracious. I think we came into action about a dozen times – rearguard action the

whole way through. [We were] absolutely exhausted. We were
thoroughly hungry and I don't think we were capable of any
reasonable further movement. There was only one thing that
kept us going and that was the knowledge that we were fighting
for our lives.[81]

In the late afternoon I Corps had gone into its allotted billets along the
eastern side of the Forest of Mormal. However, the advanced elements of
the German *III* and *IV Corps* had managed to infiltrate their way behind
the retreating British troops and had come into contact with 2 Division at
Landrecies and elsewhere. These engagements effectively put paid to any
prospect of I and II Corps linking up as planned that night.

In the meantime, 3 and 5 Divisions had also begun during the late
afternoon to reach their destinations to the west and east of Le Cateau,
although both 7 Brigade, which formed the rearguard to 3 Division, and
4 Division itself were still actively engaged and in contact with enemy
forces until late in the evening. Half of the cavalry corps had become
scattered during the day's fighting and manoeuvring, and would thus be
out of position for what was planned as another day of retreating on the
26th. The fact that many of Smith-Dorrien's forces were late in arriving
at their allotted positions on the night of 25/26 August would have
profound consequences for the course and conduct of the retreat. II
Corps was, in any case, in a much worse position than I Corps. It had
sustained well over 4,000 battle casualties so far over three days of hard
fighting, and its retreat had been much more difficult than that of its
sister corps as the Germans were much hotter on their heels.

In accordance with Sir John French's plans for the continuation of the
retreat on the following day, troops from II Corps had pushed out feelers
to their right in order to make contact with Haig's force, ensuring there
was no gap between I and II Corps. As a result of the decisions Haig
made later that evening to stay put until the morning, no such contact
was made, leaving unguarded the right flank of II Corps. I Corps would
in fact pull away altogether from II Corps in the morning of the 26th.
French had rightly taken the view that the only way he could keep his
small force intact and therefore effective was to create a safe distance
between it and the enormous German army bearing down upon it. With

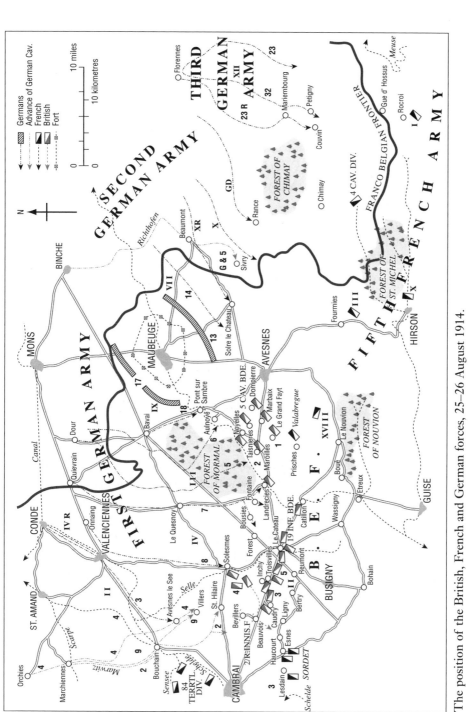

The position of the British, French and German forces, 25–26 August 1914.

good reason, he considered Lanrezac and the French forces to the east to be unreliable and unpredictable, and he was not prepared to base the safety and security of the entire BEF on the assumption that the French Fifth Army would make a serious attempt to protect the flanks of the British Army. To the left of the BEF the weak French Territorial divisions and a French cavalry corps under General Sordet (whose whereabouts were far from clear) were not considered likely to offer much resistance either. In French's view, hard marching was the only way to escape the entrapment that would inevitably result if he tried to stand and fight it out on his own.

Perhaps inevitably, the chaotic situation effectively ruled out any chance of French's orders to I and II Corps being carried out in the way he intended. The fighting that erupted between Haig's exhausted troops and the German *III* and *IV Corps* around Landrecies and Maroilles at dusk that evening had effectively ruled out French's plan for the two corps to come together. It also created a gulf between the two corps that would widen still further the following morning. German forces had made their way along the good east–west lanes that cut across the Forest of Mormal and surprised 4 (Guards) Brigade, part of 2 Division, at Landrecies. The Guards had no idea that the Germans were so close. In fact, the Germans were every bit as surprised by this chance encounter as the British. With enemy forces manoeuvring in such close proximity contact like this was almost inevitable. But it was an accidental collision and as a consequence created the maximum of confusion. The haphazard fighting continued for several hours with neither side knowing the true nature of the force they had encountered or what each other's intentions were. Combat only came to an end in the early hours of the next morning when British howitzers were wheeled into the front line and opened fire at close range. The Germans made the sensible decision to retire in the face of this onslaught and wait for reinforcements to arrive before resuming their advance at daylight.

Not unreasonably perhaps, given all that had happened so far, Haig appeared to assume the worst. According to the diary of General Charteris, Haig's head of intelligence, he at one point felt that the end might be near:

> DH ordered the whole town [Landrecies] to be organised for
> defence, barricades to meet across the roads with furniture and
> anything else handy, all secret papers etc to be destroyed. He
> sent me off to prepare a big school building for defence, giving
> me a couple of companies of Guards as a working party. For
> once he was quite jolted out of his usual placidity. He said, 'If
> we are caught, by God we will sell our lives dearly.'[82]

Although the fighting posed a serious threat to Haig's headquarters, the
capture of which would have been a disaster for the British, it was not
particularly heavy, with around 100 casualties on each side. Haig's main
fear was probably that the Germans had cut off his line of retreat. So,
instead of following his orders to link up with II Corps, Haig felt his only
course of action now was to retire towards the south, and not the south-
west as French had indicated in his orders issued on 25 August, opening
up in the process a separation between himself and Smith-Dorrien. This
was the second time that Haig had ignored orders from GHQ on the
conduct of the retreat, although to be fair, during the course of those few
confused hours of fighting at Landrecies, GHQ also came to the same
view about this new line for I Corp's retreat.

In truth, neither Haig nor Smith-Dorrien had much confidence in Sir
John French's ability as a commander, a fact which did not bode well for
the conduct of operations at this critical stage of the war. Nor would it
provide the necessary foundations of trust and confidence when things
began to go wrong. Before the BEF had even left for France, Haig had
noted in his diary on 11 August that he:

> had grave doubts, however, whether either [French's] temper
> was sufficiently even or his military knowledge sufficiently
> thorough to enable him to discharge properly the very difficult
> duties which will devolve upon him during the coming
> operations with Allies on the Continent. In my own heart I
> know that French is quite unfit for this great command at a
> time of crisis.[83]

Charteris confirmed Haig's view in his own diary in an entry made on 18
August:

DH unburdened himself today. He is greatly concerned about the composition of British GHQ. He thinks French quite unfit for high command in time of crisis. He says French's military ideas are not sound; that he has never studied war; that he is obstinate and will not keep with him men who point out even obvious errors.[84]

Smith-Dorrien was a latecomer to the BEF, having been appointed to lead II Corps only after the sudden death on 7 August of Sir John Grierson, an old friend and ally of Sir John French. French had asked for Hubert Plumer to be appointed in Grierson's place, only for Kitchener to immediately overrule him in favour of Smith-Dorrien. It was a decision that did nothing to improve relations between the two men, which had famously turned sour back in 1907 when Smith-Dorrien succeeded French as the commander at Aldershot. Smith-Dorrien was an infantry man, French a cavalry diehard. Smith-Dorrien soon began to unpick many of French's ways of doing things at Aldershot and French was furious with him for doing so. The antipathy between the two was well known throughout the army.[85]

Tom Bridges had a similar view of the relationship between French and Smith-Dorrien:

Smith-Dorrien was sent out, a good fighting soldier but a man with whom French had never seen eye to eye. Both men were self-opinionated. This led to discord in the command. Neither Smith-Dorrien nor Douglas Haig, the two corps commanders, seem to have had confidence in the commander-in-chief and each acted apparently on his own initiative rather than on the orders he received, though their reasons for this were no doubt excellent.[86]

Haig had departed from his orders for the first time the day before. On 24 August he had been ordered to cover the retirement of II Corps from Mons. Not unreasonably, he considered this order impossible to comply with. His men were further to the east and would have to execute a flank march across the advancing German forces in order to comply with French's instructions – a move that any competent military strategist would immediately have ruled out as dangerous and foolhardy. But whatever the merits or otherwise of Haig's decision, it had the effect of leaving II Corps to face the full force of the enemy. Haig's decision to ignore GHQ's instructions for the second time meant II Corps would endure a similar experience again on the 26th. As it turned out, Smith-Dorrien would soon follow Haig's example in ignoring the views of his commander-in-chief.

As the fighting at Landrecies began to subside in the early hours of 26 August, Haig, far from being reassured, issued a series of confusing reports that could only have confirmed the strong views of the commander-in-chief that the retreat must be continued urgently. The most charitable explanation for the confusion is that Haig and his commanders on the ground knew neither the exact scope or strength of the enemy nor the precise whereabouts of the main body of the enemy. Just after 1.30am Haig described the situation to GHQ as 'critical'. Two hours later he asked GHQ to tell Smith-Dorrien to extend his right flank and send reinforcements to help him at Landrecies, even though it was Haig's job to join up with II Corps, not the other way around. Smith-Dorrien politely but firmly declined to offer any such help as he was simply not in any position to oblige.

Having received these conflicting messages from Haig, GHQ naturally became thoroughly disoriented. Then Haig sent Lanrezac a message reporting that I Corps had been violently attacked and was retiring on Guise, ie to the *south* or if necessary *south-east* but that the general retreat would continue in a *south-westerly* direction. Even the best commanded army cannot retire in three different directions at the same time. Chaos reigned. Fortunately for Haig and I Corps, however, the real danger to the BEF lay on its left flank and not on its right.

While French and Haig panicked in the early hours of the 26th, Von Kluck's First Army, consisting of seven infantry corps and a cavalry corps, was breathing down the neck of Smith-Dorrien's II Corps. The German *II Cavalry Corps* together with *IV Corps* were within touching distance of Le Cateau as dawn broke on the 26th, with the *IV Reserve Corps* only a short march behind. The *III Corps* was fast approaching from the east. Smith-Dorrien, acting in accordance with the strict instructions he had been given, intended to continue his retreat on the morning of the 26th and had issued orders to that effect at 10.15 on the evening of the 25th, with the transports to leave at 4am and the main bodies of 3 and 5 Divisions at 7am.

During the course of the night, however, he had become increasingly concerned that the units tasked with the responsibility of protecting the corps' vital left flank would find it impossible to carry out his orders. General Allenby, commanding the cavalry corps, was the first to voice his concerns about the overall situation. Allenby had been ordered by French to cover the retirement of II Corps by holding the high ground to the north and west of Le Cateau. Allenby had not received these orders until after much of this ground, particularly to the north of Viesly, had already been ceded to the enemy. Allenby did not have the force necessary to retake it. Only one of his brigades was available for this task, which would not have been enough to dislodge the Germans who had now arrived in strength. Whether they held the high ground or not, his cavalry brigades were in any case so scattered that it was unlikely they could provide much cover at all. Allenby told Smith-Dorrien that the Germans were virtually upon them, and unless the troops of II Corps could move off before daylight, they would be caught by the enemy and forced to fight.

Even as Allenby and Smith-Dorrien were conferring, the troops of 3 Division were still arriving in their positions at Le Cateau. Many of them had been marching and fighting all day. Smith-Dorrien now asked Hubert Hamilton, commanding 3 Division, whether it was possible for all of his troops to move off before dawn broke, but Hamilton insisted that the earliest his troops could get away would be about 9am, by which time the Germans would be already attacking. Smith-Dorrien took the immediate decision to cancel his orders for the retreat; II Corps would stand and fight instead. 'Very well, gentlemen,' he was recorded as saying, 'we will fight and I will ask General Snow to fight under me as well.'

His plan, hurriedly conceived and communicated to many units of II Corps only moments before the fighting started, was to deliver a stopping blow behind which he could recommence the retirement – something that neither pre-war training nor doctrine had ever contemplated the British army doing. In fact, the 1909 Field Service Regulations, the army's training manual, more or less ruled out the sort of operation that Smith-Dorrien had in mind. Section 114 of the Regulations reads:

The guiding principle in all delaying action must be that where an enemy has liberty to manoeuvre, the passive occupation of a position, however strong, can rarely be justified and always involves the risk of crushing defeat. Under these circumstances, a delaying force must manoeuvre, so as to force the enemy to deploy as often as possible, but should rarely accept battle.

Smith-Dorrien believed that he simply had no practical alternative. Given the desperate situation in the early hours of 26 August, he felt that to continue with the retreat as planned posed a greater risk of a 'crushing defeat' than did the delaying action he had in mind. His decision to stand and fight can be seen as the act of a commander brave enough to follow his instinct rather than the rule book. It was based, at least in part, on the assumption that I Corps was guarding his right flank – something that Haig had no intention of doing, although Smith-Dorrien did not realise this until much later. Whether he would be able to execute his plan effectively, however, depended on circumstances largely out of his control, not least the weight of the German attack. When one takes all of the circumstances into account, and given the serious consequences that would inevitably follow if he got it wrong, it was one of the boldest – and most controversial – decisions taken by a British general during the whole course of the war.

As soon as he made up his mind to stand and fight, Smith-Dorrien informed GHQ of his change of plan in a lengthy message dispatched by motor car. The message arrived at GHQ in St Quentin at about 5am. A short while later Smith-Dorrien received a largely positive message of support from French:

If you can hold your ground the situation appears likely to improve. 4 Division must co-operate. French troops are taking offensive on right of I Corps. Although you are given a free hand as to method, this telegram is not intended to convey the impression that I am not as anxious for you to carry out the retirement and you must make every endeavour to do so.[87]

Smith-Dorrien, it seems, was encouraged by this signal from French, commenting 'This reply cheered me up for it showed that the Chief did not altogether disapprove of the decision I had taken, but on the contrary considered it might improve the situation.' The truth was, of course, altogether more complicated. French had one eye on posterity and the preservation of his own reputation. His carefully crafted message to Smith-Dorrien on the eve of battle conveyed the unmistakable impression that French was in fact hedging his bets in case the decision to fight at Le Cateau ended in disaster. He neither backed Smith-Dorrien nor tried to overrule him. In this sense, French's message can be considered as an abdication of command on his part. In one of the most distasteful episodes of French's career, he would later try to claim, quite falsely, that he never gave Smith-Dorrien any reason to believe he supported the decision to stand and fight at Le Cateau. Even more shamefully, and contrary to his own reports to London at the time, he later refused to acknowledge the role that Smith-Dorrien played in helping the BEF make good its retreat on the 26th. In fact, the whole campaign could all too easily have ended in disaster for the BEF if Smith-Dorrien had not decided to ignore his orders and engage the Germans in battle at Le Cateau.

Smith-Dorrien himself described the predicament he was in with masterful understatement:

> I had received orders to continue the retirement at dawn. The position of all the troops in this area was very scattered, the men were very tired, there was a very large force of the enemy in close touch with us all along the line and a very good chance of the retirement turning into a rout. The situation was not a pleasing one.[88]

Smith-Dorrien was right about the condition of his men. Jack Tyrell, a private in the 1st Duke of Cornwall's Light Infantry, 14 Brigade, 5 Division, graphically described the situation:

> I've never been so tired and that went for the rest of us. We had been on the go for what already seemed like weeks. There had been quite a few casualties and some of the older ones had fallen out on the line of march. But especially I remember being hungry and thirsty. I don't think we had had a square meal for two days and just when we got to Le Cateau and thought we were

in for a rest and some grub, we were sent on to a ridge across the river [Selle]. There I sat down and in no time at all I was asleep.[89]

There were thousands of 'Jack Tyrells' at Le Cateau. His unit had been sent to the high ground to the east of Le Cateau to link up with I Corps, but for reasons that are now apparent, this never happened. As a result, the DCLI men would find themselves in a lot of difficulty as the fighting erupted in the early hours of 26 August.

Major Davis, serving with the Royal Artillery, confirmed Private Tyrell's account of the retreat that night:

Well, it was just one long drudge and the poor infantry – they had their ten minutes' rest every hour and the moment the halt was called they just threw themselves down where they happened to be standing and from being asleep on their feet they were asleep on their backs by the side of the road, even at times encroaching on the road making it extremely difficult for our vehicles not to run over their legs. In fact on one or two occasions this actually happened … We knew we were on the retirement but we had never envisaged that a thing like this could happen to us. All our pre-war training, well, was against it and morale was beginning to wane a good deal.[90]

In addition to the heat and the endless marching, the men endured hunger and thirst, as bringing up supplies was extremely difficult. Many of the men at Le Cateau began the fight that day in a state of exhaustion and desperate hunger.

Corporal William Holbrooke, of the 4th Royal Fusiliers, recounted his own experiences during the retreat from Mons when the supply wagons would,

dump these boxes of biscuits and bully on the side of the road and the first battalion back got the lot so the ones in the rear of the retreat got nothing much. Some of the villagers that were still left gave us some bread but we didn't have nothing else. We always said during the retreat from Mons we existed on green apples.[91]

The problems were even more intense for elements of the cavalry. Sergeant Ernest White of the 18th Hussars in Tom Bridges' 2 Cavalry Brigade remembered that 'for 36 hours after Mons we had no food at all. The iron ration had gone before that on the retreat. It was some time before any supplies came to us. We were eating turnips from the fields.'[92]

Lance-Corporal Victor Botting was serving with the 5th Lancers in 3 Cavalry Brigade. In the early hours of 26 August the men of his unit had been woken from their slumbers at 3.30 and ordered to make their way towards the right flank of II Corps: 'We moved away without food. Our rations were thrown at us. Some caught them, others failed.'[93] Not everyone was able to supplement their meagre rations. Corporal Fred Atkinson of the 1st Royal West Kents in 13 Brigade, 5 Division, had a much harder time en route to Le Cateau. The orchards by the side of the roads made him and his comrades feel even hungrier: 'We wanted to get hold of that fruit but you know it was forbidden, we daren't do it.'[94]

Lieutenant Money, serving with the 1st Cameronians, arrived with his battalion at the railway station in Le Cateau late on the evening of 25 August. It would not be a comfortable night: '[There were] very lumpy cobbles on which we were required to lie down. One really couldn't sleep on them, they were too much. People really just walked about for most of that night and couldn't get much rest.'[95]

The British position at Le Cateau has variously been described as a 'flattened horseshoe'[96] and a 'tipped-up, reversed L'.[97] The line held by II Corps extended for about 10 miles east to west, while 19 Brigade formed the corps reserve on the right at Reumont. The cavalry brigades were mainly spread out towards the right rear, with one weak brigade behind 4 Division on the left. The right of the line was held by 5 Division, which was crammed into the angle formed by the 'L'. Meanwhile 3 Division held the centre, with 8 and 9 Brigades occupying the high ground overlooking the village of Inchy, and the exhausted 7 Brigade further to the rear at Caudry. Out on the left was 4 Division, bending back to form a refused flank around Esnes. The men of 11 Brigade were in position at Fontaine au Pire, and those of 12 Brigade at Longsart, with Elkington, Mainwaring, Haldane and 10 Brigade at the rear in the vicinity of Haucourt and Esnes.

Unlike Mons, the position taken by II Corps at Le Cateau was in fact perfect for a defensive battle. Smith-Dorrien had possession of all the

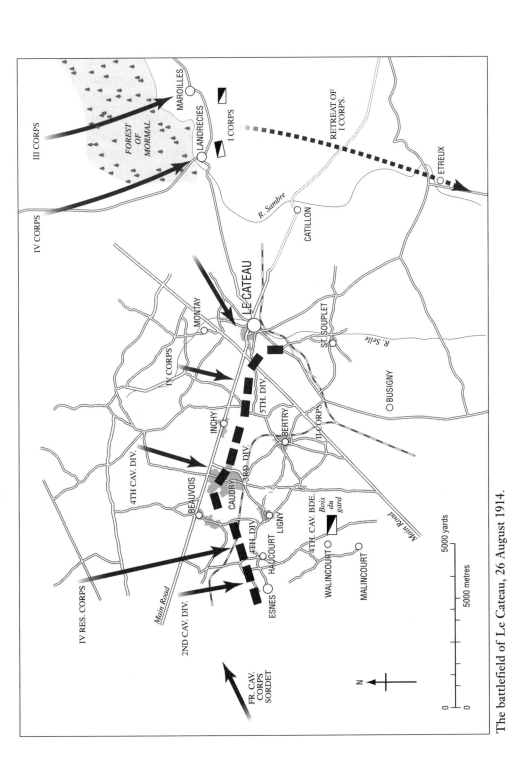

The battlefield of Le Cateau, 26 August 1914.

ridges and spurs of high ground in the centre of his line of defence, from which his men would be able to lay down fire on the enemy. The defenders also had a good field of fire across the open and undulating countryside. But Smith-Dorrien's flanks were largely unprotected and it would be on the right and left flanks, not in the centre, where the greatest danger threatened as dawn broke on 26 August. Above all, the Germans enjoyed an overwhelming superiority in men and materiel. And the attackers would enjoy one final vital advantage – surprise.

Neither Elkington nor Mainwaring had much idea of these wider tactical or strategic developments as they led their men back from St Python to Haucourt. The situation which confronted both battalions at dawn on 26 August was identical to that faced by Jack Tyrell and the Duke of Cornwall's Light Infantry. Mainwaring himself described the moment his battalion arrived in the vicinity of Haucourt along the sunken road from Ligny:

> Finally we arrived at Haucourt at about 5am. I sent the adjutant to seek for orders. He returned to say that there was no sign of the brigade staff but that he had seen Colonel Edmunds of the divisional staff who said we were to march again at 7am, another 12 miles. I went to Colonel Edmunds myself and he confirmed the order, adding that the men were to consume their iron ration, and asking me if the men could do it. I replied they could, after a couple of hours' rest and some tea.

Sadly for Mainwaring and his men, there would be no tea that day – nor indeed for some time to come.

The Royal Warwickshires had arrived at Haucourt half an hour before the Royal Dublin Fusiliers. Elkington had ordered his men to bivouac in a cornfield on the side of the road, just to the east of the village, facing the gentle slopes of the Warnelle Ravine to the north. The men took off their equipment and began to brew up. Elkington also expected that his men would be able to snatch some very necessary rest before resuming their march to new positions at Le Catelet away to the south-west.

Elkington and Mainwaring were unable to establish contact with Haldane was because he was out scouting the ground in front:

As I rode up the ridge which overlooks Haucourt from the north, I found the outposts of the 12th Brigade engaged in digging a trench in a beetroot field some way down the forward slope. I went on to the village [Haucourt] and at the Mairie found General Snow who told me that my brigade had shortly before arrived, having lost touch with the transport near Beauvais owing to the pace at which it was moving. He desired me to come with him in his motor car and look at the position which he proposed to hold, for Sir Horace Smith-Dorrien to whose Army Corps 4 Division was attached had decided that he must stand and fight as his own divisions – 3 and 5 – were too exhausted to march further.[98]

Haldane had witnessed another curious sight that morning: 'There passed across my front, in solemn procession, a French dragoon regiment, still wearing cuirasses and shining brass helmets, moving towards Cambrai, and one could not help thinking that our allies were in military dress terms at least, several decades behind us.'[99] These French cavalrymen were part of Sordet's cavalry corps, which would play an important part later that day in helping extricate 4 Division from the battlefield.

Snow had arrived at the Mairie earlier that morning and set up his headquarters there. He had also been trying to grab some sleep when he was wakened with news that II Corps would stand and fight after all. Detailed orders were prepared for the defence of 4 Division's positions. Unfortunately, there would be no time for these orders to reach any of his units. Snow was anxious, however, to see at first hand the position his division would have to defend. Snatching a cup of tea and an egg for breakfast, he ran out into the courtyard of the Mairie and commandeered a nearby staff car, before heading off towards Cattenieres with Haldane sitting alongside him in the rear seats. En route they had a lucky escape. Their driver overshot a junction, and as he was turning the car around, the road they should have been following was suddenly swept by heavy machine-gun fire and shrapnel. Snow recalled:

At the same time I saw shells bursting all along the position and a good many stragglers began coming back from the ridge. Haucourt village was also being shelled as we left the car and

walked across the field to a grove of trees west of Haucourt.
There we met Captain Allfrey who told me that the rumour was
that I had been killed and that General Milne [Divisional
Commander of Artillery] had taken command. Gradually the
staff rejoined me and we got an order placing the division under
the command of II Corps.[100]

The troops that Haldane had earlier seen digging in on the forward slopes
of the Warnelle Ravine were men of the 1st Battalion, King's Own Royal
Lancasters, part of 12 Brigade. They had absolutely no idea they were
under direct observation from German machine-gunners less than 800
yards away, hidden in the outskirts of Cattenieres. Soon the machine-guns
opened up a deadly burst of concentrated fire on the men from
Lancashire. Hundreds of them became casualties in minutes, including
their commanding officer, who was killed. German field artillery added to
the horrendous predicament of the Royal Lancasters when it commenced
firing from positions at Wambaix further to the north-west. The battalion
was a sitting duck, as near perfect a target for the German gunners as it is
possible to imagine. Carnage reigned for several minutes before frantic
efforts were made to extract the survivors from their exposed positions in
the beetroot field.

Elkington and Mainwaring would soon be in the thick of things.
Elkington described the scene vividly: 'No sooner had the men taken off
their equipment and were getting ready for a rest than heavy artillery fire was
heard and wagons were seen rushing down a hill opposite us and slightly to
our left, many of them being overturned.' Mainwaring also had a good view
of the opening salvoes of the battle: 'At about 6am a furious firefight broke
out on a small hill about 1,000 yards to the north-east. Suddenly a wave of
men from another corps came pouring in confusion back over the hill
towards us.' Captain Hart of the Royal Warwickshires had a similar
experience: 'a terrible sight was to be seen. Down the Cattenieres road, near
the quarry, poured the remnants of 1 King's Own, while two of their
wagons, the horses dead, lay on the side of the road just above the quarry.'[101]

Haldane was even closer to the action:

General Snow and I had gone but a short distance when heavy
rifle fire was opened apparently from the north upon the troops

on the ridge for bullets came flying over Haucourt village. What was taking place was that the German advanced guard, composed chiefly of cavalry and machine guns carried on motor cars, had surprised our outposts and the troops which were covering them and, taking them at a disadvantage, was driving them off the greater part of the ridge.[102]

Haldane was correct: 4 Division's opponents that morning were the dismounted cavalry soldiers and armoured machine-gun cars of 2 Cavalry Division under von der Marwitz, and the German forces were not only pushing 12 Brigade off the ridge but were also attempting to move around its left flank at Esnes. Mainwaring and Elkington, on their own initiative, were quick to react to the danger. Both men acted coolly and calmly. Elkington felt that the only way to help the battered Royal Lancasters was to push his men up to the top of the ridge and provide them with covering fire:

> I immediately got the battalion together. Two companies I formed up in a ditch by the side of the road just in front of us, the two remaining companies about two hundred yards in the rear. I then looked at the situation and decided that the best way to relieve the pressure was to make a counter-attack against this hill. This I did with my battalion but once having gained the top of the hill we came under heavy Maxim and shrapnel fire and I considered it necessary to fall back. I fell back slowly to my old position and entrenched.

Lieutenant Montgomery recounted how Elkington reacted to the opening salvoes:

> The CO galloped up to us forward companies and shouted to us to attack the enemy on the forward hill at once. This was the only order; there was no reconnaissance, no plan, no covering fire. We rushed up the hill, came under fire, my company commander was wounded and there were many casualties.[103]

In a letter home, Montgomery described this action as 'terrible work as we had to advance through a hail of bullets from rifles and machine-guns and through a perfect storm of shrapnel fire. Our men behaved very well though they were knocked down like nine-pins.'

As the company attack went in, Captain Hart found Elkington on the Haucourt–Ligny road:

> I was informed that he was attacking the ridge … and was ordered to take my men forward. The leading companies had got well up the hill before those in rear had got more than two-thirds of the way up and were already being driven back under artillery, machine-gun and rifle fire.[104]

Private Hill took part in this attack:

> Our eager young officers went frantic with excitement. On their own initiative they led us up the hill to the rescue of our comrades. With wild shouts we dashed up. At first the ground was broken and afforded cover for our short sharp dashes. We then came to a hedge with a gap of about 4 yards wide. A dozen youngsters made for the gap, unheeding the advice of older soldiers to break through the hedge. Soon that gap was a heap of dead and dying as a machine-gun was trained on it. We reached an open field where we were met with a hail of shrapnel. Officers were picked off by snipers. A subaltern rallied us and gave the order to fix bayonets. A piece of shrapnel carried half his jaw away.
>
> Upwards we went but not a sign of a German. They had hidden themselves and waited for our mad rush. Officers and sergeants being wiped out and not knowing where the enemy was really, our attack fizzled out. A staff officer came galloping amongst us on a big black charger. He bore a charmed life. He shouted something unintelligible which someone said was the order to retire.
>
> The survivors walked slowly down puzzled and baffled. They had attained nothing and had not even seen the men they set out to help.[105]

The battalion war diary records a total of 7 officers and 40 other ranks becoming casualties in these attacks. Although the men had got to the top of the ridge, it was impossible to hold the high ground under the weight of enemy fire. They had, however, perhaps unknown to Private Hill, been able to provide some covering fire for the beleaguered Royal Lancasters. As a result, the soldiers of one company were then able to leave the ridge in relative safety and come back down the reverse slope with the Warwickshires, where they joined forces with Elkington's men. Here they would remain for the rest of the day, fighting alongside their rescuers.

At the same time as 10 and 12 Brigades came under fire, 11 Brigade, on the right of the division's front, was dealing effectively with an incursion of German infantry into and through Fontaine au Pire. Here the 1st Hampshires had destroyed a platoon of *Jager* with accurate rifle fire. After this brief exchange of fire, the Germans made no attempt to push any further.

The *Official History*, rather strangely, describes another two-company attack said to have been launched by Elkington's men against the Germans on the crest of the ravine later that morning at 8.45am. There is no reference to this in the battalion's own war diary and no surviving personal account confirms that such an attack took place at all.

These accounts show Elkington as a decisive and brave commander. He made an instant assessment of the danger faced by the troops in front of him and responded with calm, clear orders. Struggling as he must have been with the physical effects of the last few days, he rose manfully to the occasion. Curiously, however, the *Official History* blanks out Elkington's role in this action altogether, claiming that the order to attack the ridge was issued by a 'staff officer'.[106] This was clearly not true. At this time the Royal Warwickshires were not in touch with either brigade or divisional headquarters, and Elkington himself was the author of the attempt to come to the aid of the Royal Lancasters on the ridge. Conspiracy theorists may make what they will of this curious error in the *Official History*, an error made even more puzzling by the fact that the author was none other than Colonel Edmonds, who was on the staff of 4 Division and was present at the Mairie in Haucourt at the time of the attack.

After this opening action, it is clear from Elkington's account that he remained in the battalion's front line, no more than 300–400 yards from the village of Haucourt itself.

Mainwaring was also stirred into action as the fighting started, although not in quite the same way as Elkington. The Royal Dublin Fusiliers, to the right of the Royal Warwickshires along the Ligny road, deployed to face the expected enemy infantry attack coming down the Warnelle Ravine. Mainwaring recalled: 'I fell in the battalion and directed Captain Clarke to extend his company along the road facing the firing and Captain Higginson to do the same, slightly in echelon behind Captain Clarke, and left Major Shewan in charge of these companies.'

Captain Higginson's D Company took up a position close to a large round tower on elevated ground to the south of Haucourt. This gave them excellent observation over the ground in front, but the tower would serve as a marker for German artillery fire. Mainwaring had wanted the other two companies to take up a defensive position behind the two forward companies deployed along the Ligny road and on the higher ground close to the tower. However, for some reason the rearward movement of these two remaining companies had gone too far, and Mainwaring was eager to correct their mistake. Unfortunately his own horse had been taken away for watering shortly before the firing had started, and it was some time later before he was able to ride after his two wayward companies and halt their retreat along a cart track that linked Haucourt to Caullery, another small hamlet a mile and a half to the south-east. By this time the two companies had moved back about 1,000 yards from the front line. Mainwaring would remain at this position for most of the fighting, largely out of contact with the battalion, the brigade and the battle itself. His decision to stay here rather than returning to his men in the front line would have serious implications later on, and would contribute to the battalion losing all cohesion in the later stages of the battle.

Captain Watson, the battalion adjutant, recounted these initial movements of the Royal Dublin Fusiliers:

> I was with Colonel Mainwaring and we remained for a short time with A and D companies whilst he gave instructions to the officers. The other two companies had in the meantime gone towards Caullery. I ran after them and finally they took up positions about 800 to 1000 yards north of the village.[107]

Captain Wheeler, commanding C Company, confirmed these events in an account written on 4 September:

> At about 6.15am on August 26 the battalion was formed in mass north-east of Haucourt when gunfire was opened from the high ground north of that place. The battalion moved in a southerly direction in artillery formation to take up a new position. After crossing the Ligny–Haucourt road, A and D Companies and one platoon of B Company were extended to form a firing line and supports, the remaining companies forming a reserve position. C Company was ordered to watch the right flank.[108]

It is clear from all these accounts of the first few minutes of fighting at Haucourt that Mainwaring was in effective command of his battalion and made sensible decisions under fire. Both Elkington and Mainwaring had split their battalions in a standard disposition, with two companies of each battalion taking up forward positions and the other two companies in reserve. However, as the war diary of the Royal Dublin Fusiliers reveals, not everything went according to plan: 'Owing to two nights' strenuous work, men were extremely tired and many of them discarded part of their equipment on coming under fire.'[109]

Like Elkington, Mainwaring was very much on his own, out of touch with Haldane and his immediate chain of command. Captain Wheeler observed, 'At this time the battalion was not in touch with 10 Infantry Brigade. The position of the battalion was sent to 4 Division who approved.'[110] And Captain Watson corroborated Wheeler's account of the situation: 'We got into communication with 4 Division but although we made repeated efforts to get into contact with 10 Infantry Brigade, failed to do so.'[111]

This failure to communicate with Brigade HQ was not entirely unsurprising as Haldane, unlike Snow at the Mairie, had not yet had the chance to properly set up his own headquarters. He had been whisked away by the divisional commander for an immediate inspection of the division's front. At some point during the morning Haldane had established his headquarters at the village of Selvigny, 2 miles to the south of Haucourt, which was some distance away from his front-line battalions. It was hardly an ideal place to establish a brigade headquarters.

Anyone trying to get to Selvigny would have been spotted almost immediately by German artillery observers, thereby running the risk of attracting artillery fire. Neither Elkington nor Mainwaring had any idea that this was where their Brigade HQ had been located. It is clear from their own accounts of the day that they had absolutely no idea where Haldane was throughout the 12 hours or so the fighting lasted.

Snow himself would later that morning move his own Divisional HQ from the Mairie in Haucourt village, as it was not safe for him to remain there:

> The next move was to try to get more to the rear as the place where we found ourselves was hardly the right place for Divisional HQ. It was not easy to get further back as I did not want the troops to see the GOC making his way among the stragglers to the rear. However, by moving first towards one flank and [then] the other I gradually got back to a place just west of Caullery which did very well, but owing to the absence of my signal company every message had to be carried by one of my staff, who already had their hands full.[112]

To add to the difficulties, Captain Frankland of the Royal Dublin Fusiliers, Haldane's Staff Captain and one of his key interlocutors with the brigade's infantry battalions, had himself gone walkabout almost as soon as battle had commenced:

> When I left General Haldane shortly after an outburst of heavy shell fire, I went over to the Dublins and found them getting on all right. I then walked over to Caullery. There I collected about 50 men of different regiments and formed them into a company. With this I guarded the northern exits of the village against the anticipated advance of enemy from Ligny.[113]

Frankland clearly confirmed the impression that the Royal Dublin Fusiliers were being effectively commanded by Mainwaring at this point. Frankland's movements from this point onwards are not at all clear. His own personal account gives the sense that he remained at Caullery until about 6pm. Haldane, however, refers to Frankland being with him at certain points in the day.

There is strong evidence to suggest that a company of the Royal Dublin Fusiliers also joined in the attack on the ridge during the initial stages of the fighting, although Mainwaring himself did not order this attack and appears to have been unaware it had happened. The battalion war diary also makes no reference to it. The evidence for this attack comes from Captain Clarke, commanding A Company in the front line along the Ligny road, who later wrote a personal account of the battle:

> I met a staff officer belonging to the brigade on our right [11 Brigade] who said, 'They are very hard pressed on that ridge and my brigadier wants support. The right of your brigade are going to reinforce. Can't you take up your company?' Telling him I would see if I could, I hurried across to the second-in-command, Major Shewan, and gave him the message. He gave me leave to take up my company and said the other front company would come forward to hold my trenches and give us covering fire if we needed it. My company then rapidly advanced. The enemy got the ridge before we could reach it and drove our troops off it. So the company was ordered to retire and came back to its original position with the loss of two wounded.[114]

Perhaps this is the mysterious 'staff officer' referred to in the *Official History*, which thus may have confused what appear to have been two separate attacks by two different battalions on the ridge. It is very likely that the second counter-attack on the ridge, which is attributed in the *Official History* to the Warwickshires, was in fact this attack by the Royal Dublin Fusiliers.

Captain Clarke's account of this attack is backed up by Captain Hart, who took part in the attack by the Warwickshires: 'A company of the 2nd Royal Dublin Fusiliers and some men of the Royal Irish had joined the attack, coming from I know not where.'[115] Lieutenant Macky of the Royal Dublin Fusiliers, who would eventually end up several days later in Holland, where he was interned by the Dutch authorities, also corroborated the attack on the ridge by men of his battalion: 'I was myself leading my platoon to the attack in concert with the Warwicks, but after advancing a short distance was ordered to return to my position.'[116]

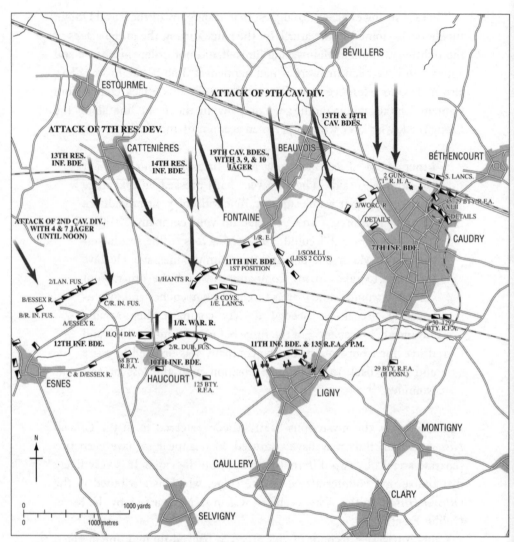

The British left flank at Le Cateau, 26 August 1914.

This initial flurry of action was over by about 10.30am. Having taken the ridge and pushed 12 Brigade south of the Warnelle Ravine, the Germans made no effort to press on with their attack. They had sustained heavy casualties themselves and needed to regroup while fresh troops were brought forward. In fact, across the whole front held by 4 Division, stout resistance had been put up by all three brigades, in particular by 11 Brigade commanded by General Hunter Weston, holding the line around Ligny. Repeated attempts to take the village had been repulsed by the steady fire of the men of the 1st Hampshires and 1st Somerset Light Infantry. The Germans had once again come face to face with the effects of concentrated, well-aimed rifle fire from soldiers who were determined to make their presence felt. Whenever they advanced against 4 Division on the morning of 26 August, the Germans suffered heavily.

However, 11 Brigade on the right was beginning to become more and more isolated from the rest of the division and also from 7 Brigade on its right. But its men held on grimly. They were under heavy artillery fire for most of the morning, but were not attacked by infantry. The situation can most accurately be described as a stand-off. German accounts of the battle describe how troops joining the fight later in the day found the cavalry on the defensive 'and several regiments were cowering under cover behind the houses'. When the reinforcements arrived to take over the front, the cavalry moved back several miles towards Cambrai to recover, a mistake which meant that at the critical moment in the battle later that evening the Germans had no forces at hand to mount a vigorous pursuit of the retiring British. The debut of 4 Division had been 'a memorable one'.[117]

General Snow was content with the first few hours of the fighting: 'When things had settled down and I could take stock of the position, I was fairly happy in my mind. I was convinced that there was nothing at present up against me except artillery and machine-guns and this I reported to HQ II Corps.'[118]

While the German cavalry waited for the infantry reinforcements to arrive, the focus of the engagement switched to a prolonged exchange of artillery fire. Here the Germans had a clear superiority. The predominantly light field artillery of the British was no match for the large numbers of German heavy guns and howitzers. German guns raked the whole length of the line held by 4 Division. In Mainwaring's words:

'By this time the action, confined in our part of the field to artillery, became general and there was nothing to be done but lie still and await the infantry attack which was momentarily expected, everyone of course being directed to dig themselves in.'

To the rear of Mainwaring's position, just behind the village of Selvigny, the howitzers of 31 Battery, Royal Field Artillery were attempting to provide 4 Division with some covering fire. Captain Pusey was serving with 31 Battery that day:

> The battery was ordered to take up a position in a cornfield, under cover of a small hill. It was whilst riding with the battery commander to the brow of this hill, which was to be the OP, that we first came under enemy artillery fire. These rounds were directed against a haystack which the Battery commander had wisely decided not to use. From the OP I could see the Battery come into action. Sheaves of corn were used as camouflage. The position was well covered and throughout the day it was not discovered by the enemy.[119]

All day 31 Battery provided excellent support to the division at Le Cateau. From his position on the hill Pusey could clearly see the impact his gunfire had on the enemy: 'The first view of the enemy infantry was extraordinary. A compact mass of grey-clad men advancing as if on a parade ground and into which the lydite from our howitzers blew great gaps.'[120]

At around midday Mainwaring received two messages from 4 Division's headquarters via Snow's aide-de-camp, Captain Allfrey. Riding his charger through the gunfire, Allfrey found Mainwaring on the cart track and told him, 'The General wishes you to hold on here to the end.' Then turning in his saddle, he told Mainwaring, 'General Snow told me to say that this is a personal message from him to the regiment.' Mainwaring confirmed his receipt of these orders and told Allfrey to let the general know the Royal Dublin Fusiliers would hold their ground. Later on, another 4 Division staff officer, Captain Burnett-Hitchcock, told Mainwaring, 'It's only going to be a case of long bowls, no retirement.' Mainwaring again indicated that the Fusiliers would not retire. Snow was evidently concerned about his left flank: 'I was certainly very nervous of my left flank not because I was led to expect a turning movement but because it was in the air and I imagined it much more in the air than it really was.'

During the morning two batteries of the Royal Field Artillery had unlimbered and come into action a few hundred yards to the right of Mainwaring's command post, and he detailed C Company to provide protection for the guns. They took up positions about 300 yards in front of the batteries and dug in.

Elkington, meanwhile, was still with his battalion dug in along the Ligny road. According to Captain Hart, Elkington had set up his Battalion HQ just behind the Ligny–Haucourt road, along the sunken path linking Haucourt to Caullery. Private Hill, one of the men under the command of Major Poole, recalled the next few hours sheltering in a scrape beside the road: 'A battery of our 18 pounders started to shell the ridge. Suddenly shells started falling around the guns. One direct hit and a gunner's leg fell amongst us. The battery was wiped out. Tired and worn out, we waited.'[121]

Haldane's whereabouts at this time are not exactly clear. As soon as the attack began he had left General Snow, still in his car, and walked back to Haucourt. Behind the village he found the Seaforth Highlanders and the Royal Irish. According to Haldane,

> The very wide front which my troops were holding obliged me
> to move about to keep touch with the situation. Part of the day
> I passed in the vicinity of my two battalions near Haucourt,
> coming in for a very heavy dose of shrapnel fire in the open,
> which continued at intervals for about one and a half hours,
> most of the shells bursting either high or on graze.[122]

Snow had asked Haldane to organise a reserve, and these two battalions, the Seaforth Highlanders and the Royal Irish, would provide it. They would be used later in the day to protect the division's left flank from being turned by enemy infantry. But Haldane was still out of communication with Elkington and Mainwaring, although they were in fact no more than half a mile away at most towards the east and the south-east of Haucourt. He had, however, lost at least one of the means by which he could have maintained contact with them: 'Unfortunately, when the Germans attacked our outposts, my brigade signals section had, in my absence, been thrown into the fight to maintain the ridge and the greater number were either killed or wounded.' There were other problems too, affecting Haldane's ability to command his brigade:

> The ground too, after the rain of the previous day, was very heavy and the horses of my staff and orderlies were too exhausted to move beyond a walk. The result was that practically all means of maintaining communication between headquarters of the brigade and its several battalions were at an end, and no little inconvenience was caused.[123]

Haldane was obviously annoyed and frustrated that he could not speak to Elkington and Mainwaring at such an important stage in the battle:

> I made several attempts, as did also my staff captain, to find the commanding officers of these two battalions, but the only senior officer of either battalion with whom I was able to communicate was Major Shewan [Royal Dublin Fusiliers] who did not himself know where the Commanding Officer was.[124]

Captain Frankland, the staff captain referred to by Haldane, was, as we know, in Caullery for at least some part of the day, 2 miles to the rear of Haucourt. Frankland makes no reference in his account of the day's fighting to any attempt to contact Mainwaring or Elkington, and there is certainly no mention that he succeeded in doing so. But Haldane is quite clear that Frankland was with him for much of the time and that during the middle of the afternoon had made further attempts to get into contact with the Dublin Fusiliers and Royal Warwickshires. Mainwaring himself was only a few hundred yards away from Frankland along the cart track to Haucourt and would not have been hard to find. It is true that Elkington was further away from Caullery, just behind the Haucourt–Ligny road, although Frankland must have passed through the Royal Warwickshires during his early morning trip to visit the Dublin Fusiliers and he therefore knew at least where to look. The two battalions were, after all, entrenched along the very same road.

This breakdown in communication had a profound effect on Haldane, and it is likely that he attributed to it much of the blame for what happened later, in particular the disintegration of his brigade during the early evening. It is repeatedly mentioned in his personal accounts of the fighting, and also featured heavily in a note entitled 'Retirements' that he wrote to inform brigade practice a few weeks later:

> I impress on commanding officers the importance of keeping in close touch with their brigade headquarters so that orders to retire can readily be issued. And on officers in command of troops the danger that may result in their withdrawing until ordered to do so. Should it appear that a retrograde retirement is in progress, an officer in command of troops should take every possible step to ascertain what is required of him – if orders have not reached him – *before taking upon himself* the responsibility of retiring. No vague or doubtful order to retire should be acted upon.[125]

The tone of this very interesting note, particularly its reference to commanding officers acting without brigade authority, undoubtedly reflected Haldane's experiences on 26 August. In truth, it reads as both a description of events on that fateful day and a thinly veiled criticism of the actions of his subordinate commanders. It also reveals very clearly what Haldane felt lay at the heart of the difficulties his brigade encountered as the fighting progressed on 26 August and where he felt the blame should correctly lie.

As the fighting erupted on their own brigade front, Haldane, Elkington and Mainwaring were all naturally focused on their own immediate predicament, and largely unaware of what was happening elsewhere along the line held by II Corps. In fact, in the centre of the British line there had been little pressure during the morning. German infantry had been spotted several thousand yards away, but made no concerted effort to attack. The village of Caudry had been heavily shelled from about the same time as the Royal Lancasters were attacked on the Warnelle Ravine. The British infantry, ably supported by the artillery, easily kept at bay their opponents, who did not press their attacks here with any great strength or determination but were instead focusing their efforts on the flanks of Smith-Dorrien's force.

On the right of the line of II Corps it had been a very different story. German *IV Corps* infantry moved into the eastern outskirts of Le Cateau early in the morning and ambushed Jack Tyrell and his comrades, who were forced back on to the high ground to the south-east of Le Cateau. German troops then began advancing down the mist-covered valley of the Selle and also took up positions on the valley's high eastern banks; from this important vantage point enfilade fire from German batteries would eventually be directed along the whole length of the British line. These initial movements would spell real trouble for 5 Division later in the day, and indeed for the entire British position at Le Cateau. For several hours the fighting raged on. The British positions all around the village of Le Cateau were subjected to heavy artillery fire, which took a murderous toll on the infantry as well as the gunners.

The 2nd Suffolks and 2nd King's Own Yorkshire Light Infantry in particular, dug in on high ground protecting the crossroads to the west of Le Cateau, were directly in the path of the main German thrust on the right flank. A young officer with the KOYLI, Lieutenant Butt, recalled his chilling instructions on this fateful day: 'The COs were summoned and the positions explained. The brigade was to be sacrificed to save the 5th Division. Our orders in the regiment were that we had to stay and fight it out to give the Division more time to get clear.'[126]

Here the fighting was intense and deadly, with casualties high on both sides. Extraordinary acts of bravery and heroism were commonplace. For several frenetic hours these two battalions, supported by over 40 field guns and a heavy battery of howitzers, defied the full force of the German onslaught. But inevitably, the Germans' sheer weight of numbers began to give them the advantage. Although reinforcements managed to reach the Suffolks and the KOYLI, their position on the hill overlooking the crossroads began to give way in the middle of the afternoon under the remorseless pressure. Lieutenant Butt described the moment when the KOYLI could hold on no longer: 'We did our best and the Germans failed to sweep over us until, as far as I remember, 3pm. Our rapid rifle fire was always of a pretty high standard.'[127]

To the left of the KOYLI and Suffolks, men of the 1st Bedfordshires were enduring a similar experience. Among them was Sergeant Harold Spencer:

At 11am sniping commenced. At midday a colonel came along ordering 'no retirement whatever'. The German artillery soon found out our neat little trenches. The German infantry poured in on us in masses and lost very heavily. Our artillery played a fine game on them until about 5pm. Our men were badly cut up and forced to retire. The Germans were outflanking us. At this point the Germans were slow. Had they been smart they could have captured the whole lot of us.[128]

Corporal Fred Atkinson of the 1st Battalion, Royal West Kents, part of 13 Brigade, 5 Division, remembered what happened to him and his mates at about this time, after the order 'no retirement' reached them as they lay in their shallow trenches: 'it was just as though an arsenal had been showered on us. An arsenal of explosives.'[129]

At about 1pm Sir Charles Ferguson, the commanding officer of 5 Division, observing that his right was beginning to give ground, alerted Smith-Dorrien to the news that a fresh German division was working around his right flank. Unless assistance could be sent, he would be obliged to begin a general retreat. Smith-Dorrien rapidly placed two battalions from 19 Brigade at Ferguson's disposal in order to help him extricate his men from their positions. But the die was cast and Smith-Dorrien told Ferguson to begin to pull out his division as soon as he thought fit, after which 3 and 4 Divisions would also retire. The rest of the line could not be held any longer once 5 Division was forced to move back.

Ferguson's orders to retire began to reach the battalions of his division at about 3pm, confirming Lieutenant Butt's recollections. On this part of the line it was easy enough for orders to reach brigades, but it was practically impossible for them to percolate down to the battalions in the front line, given the intensity of the fighting. This was exactly the same situation as that faced by Elkington and Mainwaring over on the left flank.

The end came between 2.30 and 2.45pm. The Suffolks were overwhelmed, together with some of the Argyll and Sutherland Highlanders and the men from the 2nd Manchesters who had joined them for the final stages of the battle. They made a heroic last-ditch stand. Two officers of the Highlanders were observed calmly firing their rifles at the advancing German soldiers and counting their tallies out loud as if they were on the firing ranges at home. The Suffolks had fought for nearly 9 hours, making no effort to withdraw until ordered to do so and only then when they were under fire from their right, left and rear.

Fred Petch, a young private soldier with the 2nd Suffolks, described what happened to him around midday:

> I was firing away at some Germans trying to creep up a little gully to my right when I was hit by two machine-gun bullets. One ricocheted off the stock of my rifle but the other went through my left hip and out through my right leg which left me pretty well paralysed. There was no way anyone could move me and I was picked up later that evening by the Germans.[130]

Some years later a German officer who fought with *7 Division, IV Corps* at Le Cateau recalled the resistance offered by the Suffolks on the ridge above the crossroads:

> I did not think it possible that flesh and blood could survive so great an onslaught. Our men attacked with the utmost determination but again and again they were driven back by those incomparable soldiers. Regardless of loss, the English artillery came forward to protect their infantrymen and in full view of our own guns kept up a devastating fire.

Lieutenant Rory MacLeod of 80 Battery, XV Brigade, RFA, attached to 5 Division, described how his men behaved as they offered support to the beleaguered Suffolks and KOYLI: 'The drill throughout was admirable. All the men, in spite of the shelling and casualties, were as calm, quiet and steady as if on a gun drill parade.'[131]

An hour later a similar fate to that of 2 Suffolks' befell the men of the 2nd KOYLI, who had stood their ground in the face of enormously superior enemy forces until they were completely surrounded. They never received the order to retire and so held their ground to the end. The defiance and nerve of this exceptional battalion had won precious time for the rest of 5 Division to make good its retirement.

To the rear of 5 Division, along the valley of the Selle, elements of 1 and 3 Cavalry Brigades, supporting Jack Tyrell's Cornwall Light Infantry and the East Surreys, also helped to delay the German *III Corps* in their efforts to turn the flank of II Corps. Jack Tyrell, who was himself wounded in the arm after the first exchanges, could not believe their luck: 'I wasn't badly hurt, but I couldn't use my rifle. If the Germans had really come after us they would have eaten us alive. Why, when we got back to the main road, we even had time for a proper meal before marching off again!'[132]

By 6pm the division had broken off contact with the enemy. Largely as a result of the determined rearguard action fought by the Suffolks and the KOYLI, the German infantry had had enough. The battered troops of 5 Division were able to withdraw entirely unmolested, except for artillery fire targeted on the main road to the south. Together with the men of 19 Brigade, they were directed to move south-eastwards to St Quentin, where supplies awaited them, and then to move on to Ollezy, 4 miles to the east of Ham.

Major Geiger of the 2nd Battalion, Royal Welch Fusiliers, part of 19 Brigade, described the difficulties of this march:

> As rearguard, we marched in file with bayonets fixed. When we looked back we could see the glare in the sky of places that had been set on fire by the shelling and otherwise. The march was a painful business. Mercifully the night was cool but we were all pretty beat. The marches had not been excessive, about 20 miles on each of the first two days and about 16 miles already this day, but no one had had more than a couple of hours' sleep a night since Friday and it was now Wednesday ... consequently many of us were reeling all over the road.[133]

Regimental Sergeant-Major Boreham, also of the 2nd Battalion, Royal Welch Fusiliers, remembered one particular incident along the way:

> We managed to keep the men fairly well together though it was a bit of a job to prevent some of them falling to lie down and sleep. I saw a man fall out and wander towards the gate of a

farm we were passing. Taking hold of his arm I asked him where he was going; he looked at me with a fixed stare and mumbled that he was going to have a sleep. I pushed him back into the ranks and the movements of the other men kept him going. I am quite sure he had no idea what he was doing; his senses were numbed by want of sleep for so long.[134]

From his Corps Headquarters at Bertry, just behind the line held by these two battalions, Smith-Dorrien had a perfect view of the retreat. As the division came down the main road past him, there was severe congestion and many of the units were broken up. But there was no panic, despite the fact that the enemy were close at hand. Smith-Dorrien recorded in his diary:

It was a wonderful sight, men smoking their pipes, apparently quite unconcerned and walking steadily down the road – no formation of any sort and men of all units mixed up together. I likened it at the time to a crowd coming away from a race meeting ...[135]

In the centre, the retirement of 3 Division was made much easier by the rearguard actions fought by 5 Division. But here too, the withdrawal of the main body of troops was helped immeasurably by another act of extraordinary bravery by another fine front-line battalion, this time the 1st Battalion, Gordon Highlanders, aided by a small party from the 2nd Battalion, Royal Scots. The Scotsmen were stretched out to the right of the village of Caudry, overlooking the village of Audencourt and the Cambrai–Le Cateau road, and the order to retire never reached them. Between 5 and 6pm they stood their ground, even though they were faced by overwhelmingly superior numbers of the enemy, who were by now beginning to press home their attacks. Their indomitable defiance helped the rest of 3 Division get away in reasonable safety and under little direct pressure. On the centre and right the 'stopping blow' envisaged by Smith-Dorrien was working. The men of 3 Division were ordered to retire towards Ham, via Bellicourt, Hargicourt and Vermand, where they would join up with 5 Division.

John Elkington, pictured after the Royal Warwickshires' regimental shooting party had taken part in the Southern India Rifle Meeting held at Bangalore in 1903. The photograph was probably taken at Belgaum, where the battalion was stationed. (*Reproduced by kind permission of the Museum of the Royal Regiment of Fusiliers*)

Lieutenant-Colonel John Ford Elkington, the commanding officer of the 1st Battalion, Royal Warwickshire Regiment.

DUBLIN FUSILIERS AT YORK.

Officers of the Royal Dublin Fusiliers relaxing in York in the first few days of the war. Colonel Mainwaring is on the left, standing with his hands on his hips.

Officers of the 2nd Battalion, Royal Dublin Fusiliers, photographed at Gravesend in the summer of 1913. Colonel Mainwaring is in the centre of the front row.

Officers and men of C Company, 2nd Battalion, Royal Dublin Fusiliers, commanded by Captain Higginson (seated, centre). This photograph was also taken at Gravesend in 1913.

Elements of the Cavalry Division on the retreat from Mons, August 1914. (*IWM Q60695*)

A patrol from the 18th Hussars trying to gather information from local civilians, 21 August 1914. (*IWM Q83053*)

Men of the 4th Battalion, Middlesex Regiment resting in the main square at Mons, 22 August 1914. (*IWM Q70071*)

Soldiers of the 4th Dragoon Guards digging in, August 1914. (*IWM Q83057*)

Belgian civilians helping men of the Royal Scots Fusiliers fortify a house at Jemappes, 22 August 1914. (*IWM Q85212*)

The pave road at Fontaine au Tertre Farm, along which the Royal Warwickshires and the Royal Dublin Fusiliers marched on 25/26 August.

Men of the 1st Cameronians halt in a village to await orders during the battle of Le Cateau, 26 August 1914. (*IWM Q51479*)

Crowds outside the Whitehall recruiting office in August 1914. (*IWM Q42033*)

A crowd of new recruits waiting to receive their pay, outside St Martin in the Fields in Trafalgar Square, August 1914. (*IWM Q53234*)

Lieutenant-General Sir Douglas Haig (right), Commander of I Corps, conferring with his fellow generals. Second from the left is General Monro, commanding 2nd Division; second from the right is Haig's Chief of Staff, Brigadier-General J. Gough; and on the left is Brigadier-General Perceval of the Royal Artillery. (*IWM Q54992*)

General Hunter Weston, holding the map, photographed in June 1916 when he was commanding VII Corps. (*IWM Q736*)

Field Marshal Sir John French, centre, facing the camera, inspecting the BEF in Hyde Park, August 1914. (*IWM Q70032*)

Soldiers of the 1st Cameronians, 19 Brigade, resting during the retreat from Mons, probably on 24 or 25 August 1914. Lieutenant-Colonel Robertson, the commanding officer of the battalion, is sitting on the left, smoking a cigarette. One of his fellow officers, at far left, is searching for enemy aircraft. (*IWM Q51478*)

The Roman road at Estrees where Elkington and Mainwaring joined forces on their march to St Quentin, 27 August.

General Sir Thomas d'Oyly Snow, the commanding officer of 4 Division, August 1914. (*IWM HU98271*)

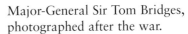

Major-General Sir Tom Bridges, photographed after the war.

Brigadier-General Aylmer Haldane, pictured while 10 Brigade was still stationed in York, August 1914.

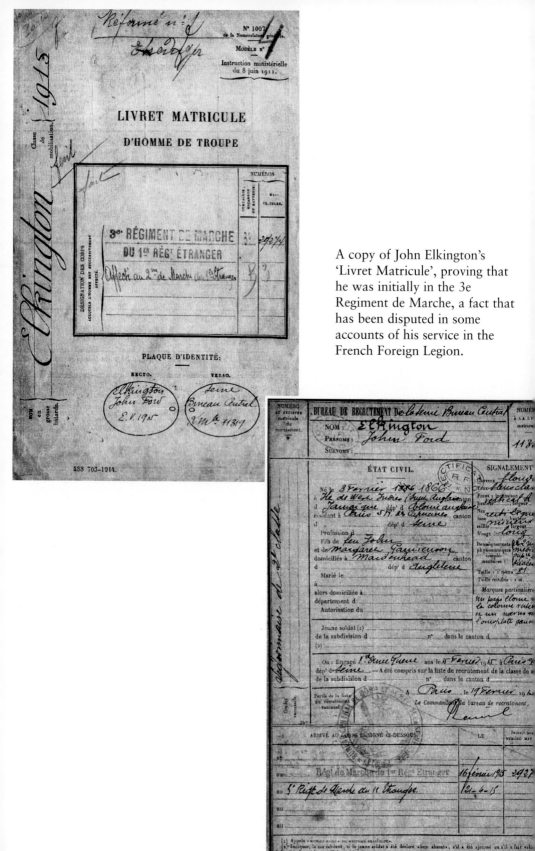

A copy of John Elkington's 'Livret Matricule', proving that he was initially in the 3e Regiment de Marche, a fact that has been disputed in some accounts of his service in the French Foreign Legion.

ACTE D'ENGAGEMENT POUR LA LÉGION ÉTRANGÈRE

L'an mil neuf cent ~~quatorze~~, le *quinze le quinze fevrier*, à *quatre* heures s'est présenté devant nous _____ Sous-Intendant Militaire résidant à Paris, département de la Seine, M *Elkington John Ford*, âgé de *quarante huit ans* exerçant la profession d _____ résidant à *Paris, 5 rue des Capucines* département de *la Seine*

Lequel nous a déclaré vouloir s'engager dans la LÉGION ÉTRANGÈRE et, à cet effet, nous a présenté :

1° Un certificat, délivré le *Quinze fevrier* par M *Raine Colonel Commandant le Bureau Spécial de Recrutement de la Seine* et constatant que M *Elkington John Ford* n'est atteint d'aucune infirmité, qu'il a la taille et les autres qualités requises pour le service de la LÉGION ÉTRANGÈRE, et que l'effectif permet de l'y admettre ;

2° Son acte de naissance constatant qu'il est né le *a déclaré ne pas posséder son acte de naissance et être né le 3 fevrier 1866 à l'Ile des West Indies (Jamaïque)*

Nous, Sous-Intendant Militaire, après avoir reconnu la régularité des pièces produites par M *Elkington John Ford* lui avons donné lecture des articles 1 et 4 de l'ordonnance du 10 mars 1831, de l'article 2 du décret du 14 septembre 1864, relatif à la durée de l'engagement, et de l'article 17 de l'Instruction sur l'admission dans la LÉGION ÉTRANGÈRE, lequel ordonne de faire conduire de brigade en brigade, par la gendarmerie, les engagés volontaires trouvés hors de la route qui leur est tracée, et de poursuivre comme insoumis ceux qui ne se rendent pas à leur destination dans les délais prescrits.

En suite de quoi nous avons reçu l'engagement de M *Elkington John Ford* _____ lequel a promis de servir avec fidélité et honneur *pendant la durée de la guerre* à partir de ce jour.

Le contractant a promis également de suivre le corps, ou toute fraction du corps, partout où il conviendrait au Gouvernement de l'envoyer.

Décret du 14 août 1906.

ART. 1er. — ~~Dans les régiments étrangers, après trois ans révolus de service, dont six mois au moins passés dans une section de discipline, le contrat d'engagement des militaires non gradés servant en Afrique étranger, pourra être résilié d'office par mesure disciplinaire.~~

ART. 2. — Les rengagements successifs contractés pour deux, trois, quatre ou cinq ans par les mêmes militaires pourront être résiliés, par mesure disciplinaire, au bout de dix-huit mois (dont huit passés dans une section de discipline) après la signature des dits rengagements.

ART. 3. — Les résiliations par mesure disciplinaire des actes d'engagement et de rengagement seront prononcées par le Général commandant le 19e corps d'armée (par le Général commandant supérieur des troupes, pour les bataillons étrangers stationnés en Indo-Chine et à Madagascar), après avis d'un conseil de discipline fonctionnant conformément au décret sur le service intérieur des corps de troupe

Indépendamment des textes susvisés et des trois articles qui précèdent nous avons également donné lecture à l'intéressé de l'article 4 (nouveau) qui fait l'objet du décret présidentiel du 24 mai 1912 et qui remplace le même article du décret du 14 août 1906.

Lecture faite à M *Elkington John Ford* il a signé avec nous,

Fred Elkington *John Fletcher* *Samuel*

Signalement de M *Elkington John Ford*

Taille d'un mètre *81* centimètres.

Cheveux *blonds*	dos *Rectiligne Sinueux*
	base _____
Yeux *Bleus clair*	Nez : hauteur _____
	saillie _____
Dents *manque 3 en haut*	largeur _____
Menton _____	Visage *long*
Poids *67 Kilogs*	inclinaison *Vertical haut*
Sourcils _____	Front : hauteur _____
	largeur _____

A copy of Elkington's attestation papers, dated 15 February 1915.

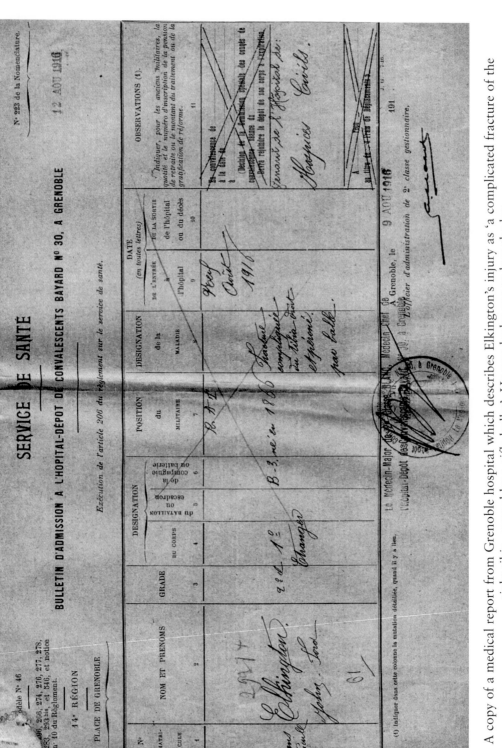

A copy of a medical report from Grenoble hospital which describes Elkington's injury as 'a complicated fracture of the right tibia, caused by a rifle bullet'. He was lucky not to lose the leg.

Over on the left, General Snow received the order to retire sometime around 4pm. The divisional war diary records some of the problems of getting orders out:

> The absence of the Signals Company rendered the control of subordinate units on a front of some 5 miles, a great deal of which was under heavy shell and rifle fire, a most difficult and arduous task, and owing to the heavy state of the ground as a result of the previous night's rain, the horses of the staff soon became tired. By the time the retirement began, it was impossible for them to direct units on the right road of retirement.[136]

This was a masterful understatement of the conditions, particularly as they affected 10 Brigade, where Elkington and Mainwaring were given no orders at all to retire, let alone what route to take. At the time these orders to retire were issued, the newly arrived infantry of the German *IV Reserve Corps* were beginning to press home the attack that had started with the slaughter of the Royal Lancasters on the slopes of Warnelle Ravine.

Over on the left flank, the initial flurry of activity around Haucourt, which saw both the Royal Warwickshires and the Dublin Fusiliers join the fight, was followed by a period of relative calm until 2pm as the enemy regrouped and prepared for a fresh onslaught. According to Mainwaring: 'I occupied the time in conference with Captain Conlon in directing the digging of trenches for details who had joined us and improving those we had already dug.'

General Snow was pleased with how his men were behaving under fire, although the difference in tactics between the two opposing armies was becoming more and more apparent:

> The men, on the whole, were behaving well. There was the usual tendency for unwounded men to help wounded men to the rear and I saw many machine-gunners wandering about in rear of the reserves saying that they were looking about for positions for their guns. This was our own fault as we had

always taught the machine-gunners to take up a position well in rear, very different to what the Germans had been taught – that the place for the machine-gun was in front of the firing line.[137]

At 2pm heavy German artillery fire opened up on the positions held by 4 Division at Haucourt and Ligny. Mainwaring found this experience particularly difficult:

> the shrapnel fire that followed was, for some two and a half hours, by common consent, something altogether out of the common. Although shrapnel does little harm in comparison with its volume, the morale effect of lying still without being able to fire a single shot in reply is very hard on even the strongest nerves.

Elkington had remained with the front two companies of his battalion all through the morning and was with them when the artillery fire began falling on his men in the afternoon. He had little comment to make about this shelling other than to record in a matter-of-fact way that, 'we stayed in these trenches all day exposed to heavy shrapnel fire during parts of the day'.

Snow described the accuracy of this gunfire: 'The thing that struck me most was the rapidity with which the German artillery got on to their target. It appeared to me as if they always got the bracket in two rounds and then the next round was plumb on the target.'

Enemy infantry followed up the artillery barrage with an advance against the left flank at Esnes, and made some progress. However, General Sordet's corps of French cavalry came into action about this time with some useful artillery support and provided reassuring protection for 4 Division's left flank. The Germans attacking the front held by 4 Division had now been reinforced by the infantry of *IV Reserve Corps*. Having fought *2* and *9 Cavalry Divisions* of the *II Cavalry Corps* to a virtual standstill earlier in the day, the men of 4 Division now faced an altogether more serious threat to their line from fresh and seasoned troops.

The fresh troops of *IV Reserve Corps* began to make their presence felt at about 4pm. At about the same time Captain Frankland, who had finally tracked down Elkington, made Haldane aware of his location:

About 3.30pm my Staff Captain [Captain Allfrey] informed me that he had found Colonel Elkington who was in the valley to the north-east of Haucourt. I proceeded in that direction when I observed that the troops who were still maintaining themselves on ground north-east of Haucourt and the valley behind them had begun a retirement apparently in the direction of Ligny. A few minutes later, possibly due to the enemy observing that some of our batteries were retiring, he opened a heavy shell fire both on them, on the troops who were still withdrawing and on the [two forward companies under Major Shewan of the] 2nd Royal Dublin Fusiliers [who were further to the east towards Ligny].[138]

Captain Hart, dug in along the Haucourt–Ligny road, remembered this time well, as he now came under artillery fire himself: 'At about 4pm the enemy turned some of his guns on to our front-line trenches and gave us about an hour's shelling, but did little if any harm.' Meanwhile, Private Hill was in the thick of things with Captain Hart in the Warwickshires' front line:

Towards afternoon shrapnel played on us, fortunately without serious result. Then it was our turn to laugh. German infantry were advancing in close formation. They broke at our first volley. Something seemed to sting my leg. I found a shrapnel bullet had ploughed a shallow groove down the fleshy part of my thigh. The enemy advanced. Another volley and they broke again. My leg began to pain me so I hobbled along the road to a house which was being used as a dressing station. A long queue of wounded men were waiting to be dressed, while a crowd of thirst-maddened unwounded were crowding round a well in the garden. Despairing of medical aid, I begged a field dressing and catching sight of a sunken road, turned into it and dressed my wound.[139]

Hill had in fact found his way into the sunken road where Elkington had established his Battalion HQ. Here he would remain until Elkington began his own independent retirement later in the afternoon.

As soon as this gunfire began, Haldane gave up trying to make contact with Elkington and instead worked his way first to a position in the rear of Haucourt village and then back to his own headquarters at Selvigny. At this point he was in effective command only of the Seaforth Highlanders and some of the Royal Irish Fusiliers. General Snow believed he received his orders to retire the division at about 2pm, although in fact it must have been later in the afternoon. He issued orders accordingly to all of his brigades.

At about 5pm Haldane received orders to form a rearguard to protect 4 Division as it moved back in what was planned to be a broadly south-westerly direction. These orders arrived via an unusual route, for it was no ordinary runner that brought them but General Wilson himself, the commanding officer of 12 Brigade, who passed them on to Haldane on his way back from the forward area.

General Snow had by now also left his headquarters to the west of Caullery. It was at this point that the situation became potentially dangerous. Haldane had had orders to act as rearguard to the division, but was struggling to comply effectively. He was out of contact with at least half of his men. Units were already mixed up and divided into smaller groups after the morning's fighting. Worse still, it seemed that many of the officers commanding these scattered forces were making their own independent decisions to retire, based on the withdrawal of the artillery, which had received clear orders to pull back. The guns of 29 Brigade, RFA, for example, had already retired to a position in the valley between Caullery and Selvigny after the torrent of enemy fire at 2pm. At about the same time 14 Brigade had moved back to a position just to the north of Selvigny. At about 4pm the howitzers of 35 Battery had been ordered to retire behind the narrow gauge railway line several miles to the rear to allow the rest of the artillery to get clear. At 4.30pm orders were issued to the Brigade Ammunition Columns to get clear and join the route of the main column at Walincourt 3 miles to the south-west of Ligny. At about 5pm both 31 and 55 Howitzer Batteries were also withdrawn to the south of Selvigny. In the absence of clear orders to the contrary, many officers, taking matters into their own hands, fell in with what they believed to be a general retirement. Haldane's plans for a rearguard action, assuming he had developed them, were already beyond rescue.

According to the *Official History*, it was 'difficult to ascertain which of the [4 Division] infantry were the first to be withdrawn'.[140] It appears that 12 Brigade on the left flank around Longsart and Esnes moved off soon after 5pm, with the 2nd Essex and two companies of the 2nd Inniskillings being the first to get away, while 11 Brigade and the remainder of 12 Brigade held their positions until 6pm or perhaps even later. Frantic and largely successful efforts were made to save the guns of 27 and 135 Batteries of 32 Brigade, Royal Field Artillery, which had been moved practically into the firing line during the day in order to support the infantry and were now coming under heavy fire.

General Snow observed one battery under fire that afternoon:

> I was watching one of our batteries near Caullery. It was under fire from about 12 guns. The enemy was firing salvoes and each salvo looked as if it must have annihilated our battery. Directly, however, the last shell of the salvo burst, bang! bang! bang! bang! bang! went the guns of the battery and you could see lanes being driven through the dense masses advancing on Ligny. Nothing could shake the defence of Ligny, whose garrison mowed down the attacking Germans literally in thousands.[141]

Despite the bravery and coolness of the troops involved, it was at this point that 10 Brigade, considered to be one of the best in the British Army, began to disintegrate as an effective unit of command. The Seaforth Highlanders and the party of Irish Fusiliers moved back with Haldane. The Warwickshires and the Dublin Fusiliers broke up into smaller parties and made their own way back at various times and in different directions during the evening.

By this time many other battalions of the division were suffering a similar fate and had also begun to break up. All of them were largely blind to the movements of their comrades, out of touch with their Brigade and Divisional Headquarters, and following no clear line of retreat. It was every man for himself. This certainly happened to the 1st Battalion, King's Own, the 2nd Inniskillings, the 1st Somerset Light Infantry, the 1st East Lancashire Fusiliers and the 1st Rifle Brigade, as well as the

Warwickshires and Dublin Fusiliers. Fortunately for all of them, the enemy showed no interest in launching a hot pursuit. German guns continued to pour a heavy fire on to the positions vacated by 4 Division, but enemy cavalry and infantry made no further appearance that evening. There is no doubt that this was in no small measure due to the heavy casualties that 4 Division had inflicted upon them. The retiring British troops were pursued by desultory gunfire but even this was easily avoided and caused few casualties.

Mainwaring made every effort to get clear orders about what he should do. He sent his adjutant, Captain Watson, with this message to Divisional Headquarters at 4.25pm:

> We have been heavily shelled for about 2 hours. The two platoons in front have suffered a good many casualties including Captain Conlon and three sergeants. These are the only troops in front of me, Captain Wheeler having retired with one company. But there are two batteries of artillery in front of me. They are not able to fire or retire. I should be glad if you could offer me advice as to what you want me to do.

According to Mainwaring, Watson returned empty handed 20 minutes later, having been unable to contact anyone at Divisional Headquarters. Mainwaring recorded what happened next:

> At about 5pm infantry which had been slowly withdrawing for some time had all passed away from the front and left front of our positions. About 5pm one of the batteries in front brought up their horses and got the guns away at full gallop. The other battery had suffered severely. We were told that two of its guns were out of action and I could see that the men could not remain behind their shields. The behaviour of our men had been splendid throughout. They were so dog-tired that many of them slept through the infernal fire as one could hear them snoring. But not one other sound of any sort did I hear during that eleven hours. The Adjutant and I were so sleepy that since it was imperative to look out for the infantry attack we determined not to fall asleep at the same time.

But now, since it was evident that there was no one left in front of us but the disabled battery, I wrote a note to General Snow, explaining the situation and asking for instructions. The Adjutant, Captain Watson, volunteered to carry it. In about 20 minutes he was back and told me that General Snow and the divisional staff had gone, that no one remained to give an order of any sort and that we were left alone.

On this information, I decided to retire and passing the word to everyone within sight to get ready, we, at about 5.30pm, retired through the village of Caullery.

There are two surprising aspects to this account. First, Mainwaring seems to have made no effort to make contact with Major Shewan's two companies in the front line, or indeed with any of his other companies nearby. Perhaps he assumed they had already retired, but if so, it is not clear on what grounds he came to this view. For a battalion commander effectively to abandon most of his companies in this way does beg some questions. Secondly, the account is contradicted by an entry in the war diary of 4 Division which records the fact that a response was made to Mainwaring's 4.25pm request for instructions: 'Order to retire sent by officer who brought this message [the 4.25pm message] by General Milne. Approved by General Snow.'[142]

General Milne was the divisional commander of artillery. It is not, however, clear from the war diary when this 'order to retire' was sent. Captain Watson's account of events adds another twist:

We were under shell-fire from 2pm onwards and about 4.45pm the guns began to go. I was sent back to try and find 4 Division, met a staff officer who said that he knew nothing about us, but as all the guns had gone, we should retire. I went back and told Colonel Mainwaring this and we retired. We had completely lost touch with the two companies in the firing line and I understood that the other companies in support had already gone.[143]

Was this 'staff officer' General Milne himself? It is likely that he would have been in or around Divisional Headquarters at this time dealing with the withdrawal of the guns, and perhaps approved the order there and then, with Snow confirming it subsequently. It is impossible to be sure one way or the other. One perfectly plausible explanation is that Mainwaring and Watson were simply mistaken about the details of events and that both their accounts are therefore unreliable on this matter. Alternatively, the war diary of 4 Division itself might be inaccurate. The order to retire could, of course, have been confirmed by either Milne or Snow later in the day, and it could be this later confirmation that is reported in the war diaries. This does not explain, however, the clear reference to Captain Watson himself, the bearer of the 4.25pm message, being given the order to retire to take back to Mainwaring. If Watson had spoken to a general officer in these circumstances it is hard to imagine he would have failed to record such a significant event. The term 'staff officer' would normally be used to refer to a less senior rank than a general. And if Mainwaring had been told that General Milne had personally approved his retirement, it is strange that this too would not have made an impact on his subsequent recollection of events.

Captain Wheeler's account confirms some of these details:

> At 4.25pm a message was sent to 10 Brigade or 4 Division for advice as to what to do owing to the infantry in the neighbourhood having withdrawn and our guns ceased firing. We were informed that the guns were being withdrawn and that we had better get away as best we could. This was done about 5.30pm, one platoon of C Company being the last infantry to leave the position.[144]

What is clear is that Mainwaring began to retire at about 5.30pm. Together with about 50 men, he moved back up the cart track to Caullery. Here he came across Captain Frankland and Major Burrowes of the Royal Irish. Together the party, in artillery formation, headed over the fields towards Elincourt, 3 miles to the south. Mainwaring was on foot, as his own horse had by now disappeared from the scene. Frankland, noticing how tired Mainwaring was, lent him his own horse and parted company with him as he headed west to Malincourt. In Mainwaring's own words, he was by now 'nearly done'. By the time he reached the village at dusk, Mainwaring had only about 40 of his men with him, as the others were simply not able to keep up with him. He got all of his men into a barn so they could at least rest while they ate their bully and biscuit, and perhaps get some sleep in the straw.

The Dublin Fusiliers had now broken up into four groups. Captain Wheeler took about 50 men with him and eventually rejoined the battalion at dawn the following day at Le Catelet, 10 miles to the south-west. Major Shewan's men would leave the front-line trenches with the Royal Warwickshires at nightfall. Company Sergeant-Major Hall found himself responsible for a group of about 100 men who must have been in and around Mainwaring's position along the cart track. They would not rejoin the battalion until 5 September. The first line transport men left under Sergeant-Major Treacher and they re-established contact with the battalion on 30 August at Carlepont.

In the meantime, Elkington faced the same dilemma as Mainwaring: when to retire and in what direction. Elkington must have been aware that troops were coming back from the front-line positions around Ligny to his right and that some kind of general retirement was already under way. According to the battalion's war diary, A Company had been ordered to retire as an escort to some guns during the late afternoon. Elkington then left Major Poole and Major Christie with the bulk of the battalion still holding the front line and withdrew with a small party of about 60 men at around 6.30pm along the road to Ligny. There is no definite explanation as to who gave the orders to A Company to retire. It is, however, clear that Elkington left the trenches he was in without informing Major Poole, who only discovered that he was on his own at about 8pm.

Elkington's own account is rather vague and to a certain extent misleading:

> Towards evening we commenced to fall back, each trench being held as long as possible, the battalion falling back in batches, we then got separated. I fell back with the men in a sunken road towards Ligny where a better position could be obtained and from there after dark we followed a main road. I did not know in which direction to retire.

Ligny was on higher ground and would therefore have given Elkington a better sense of what was going on around him than his own position at the bottom of the Warnelle Ravine. It is also true that Elkington had been given no route for his retirement. But nor had he received any order to retire. He made this decision entirely by himself. Elkington's truncated account of events at this time seems to imply that the entire battalion left the front line together as a formed body. This was certainly not the case. Elkington had in fact left most of the battalion behind him when he began to retire. His own Battalion Headquarters was some 300 yards behind Major Poole, who was commanding the two front companies entrenched along the roadside, and it seems it was from here that Elkington started his retreat, not from the front line along the Ligny road. Elkington appears to have made no effort to let Poole know that he was leaving, although he did know broadly where Poole was, having given him command of the front-line positions earlier in the day. Nor is it true to imply that the battalion was involved in fighting a rearguard action, falling back trench by trench. The Royal Warwickshires withdrew from Haucourt largely unmolested by the Germans except for some sporadic artillery fire.

Private Hill, having made contact accidentally with Battalion Headquarters as he tried to find a quiet place to dress his leg wound, retired from the sunken road with Elkington: 'In this sunken road I found Battalion HQ. At dusk they retired, I with them. Then began the retreat. I must have fainted for I remember hobbling along with some chums and next I found myself tied to the seat of an ammunition limber.'

Later that evening Major Poole, with German forces now on three sides of his position, recounted these events from a different perspective:

> After the action at Haucourt on 26 August there were left in the forward trenches and in the village about 350 men of the Royal Warwickshire Regiment, Royal Dublin Fusiliers and the Royal Irish Regiment. At about 8pm it came to my knowledge that these were all the men left and that the remainder of 4 Division had retired. As I was the senior officer I assumed command of the force and decided to withdraw and make for Selvigny, where I was informed headquarters had been during the day. I accordingly led my force away about 10pm and arrived in a village which I took to be Selvigny about 2am. There we slept. In the early morning I discovered that the village we were in was Caullery ...[145]

Captain Hart thought there were many more than 350 men in these forward trenches at the time the retirement commenced. His own estimate was much higher at around 600–700, with 300 each of the Warwickshires and Dublin Fusiliers. Captain Hart's account seems to be the most reliable.

It is worth remembering that Elkington's version of events was recounted in a statement he prepared for his court martial. His behaviour and that of Mainwaring at Le Cateau did not form any part of the charges brought against them at their subsequent court martial and so there was no reason for him to go into these events at Haucourt in any great detail. Unlike Mainwaring, Elkington clearly glossed over much more of what actually happened at Haucourt on 26 August, as well as the sequence in which it occurred. Compared to Mainwaring's much more detailed account, Elkington's statement is threadbare to say the least.

What is clear, however, is that Elkington's battalion had now been split up into three parts. A Company had left as an escort to the guns of 127 Battery. Elkington himself had left with a small party of about platoon size. The rest of the battalion remained under Poole's command. This party, using the rough and narrow cart track between Haucourt and Caullery as their escape route, stumbled back in the darkness. They could not keep together and gradually broke up into smaller groups. One of these groups was led by Major Shewan of the Royal Dublin Fusiliers. It eventually turned north and after some narrow escapes and heavy fighting managed to find its way to Boulogne several days later, although Major Shewan himself was captured by the Germans and remained a prisoner of war until the Armistice in 1918.

Major Poole's party wisely tried to avoid contact with the enemy and took a south-westerly route, marching through Malincourt, Gouy, Bony, Hesbecourt and Jeancourt, arriving at Bernes, about 10 miles to the north-west of St Quentin, on 28 August. They had to scavenge for food and water along the way, often marching at night and resting up during the day. Near Vraignes they fell in with some French cavalry, who asked for their support in an attack on some nearby German forces. They finally reached Ham later that day and fell in with the rearguard of 4 Division. According to Poole:

> The men were now very tired and straggled a good deal and
> after moving across the river [Somme] and going about another

8 or 9 miles we were put into supply wagons by order of
General Snow and were taken that night to Noyon. There the
force got split up into various detachments and went various
ways.[146]

It was painfully slow progress all the way. Captain Hart recalled the
beginning of the retreat from Haucourt:

the pace was necessarily slow, the halts long and constant and
the march seemed interminable. Tired out, most if not all slept
as they marched and several suffered from illusions brought on
by fatigue and lack of sleep. The flames from Ligny alone
lighted up and intensified the darkness of the night.[147]

Poole's men were lucky to have avoided capture along the way, and
Haldane was full of praise for the way Poole and Christie had conducted
themselves:

Major Poole and Major Christie took part in the attack on the
ridge at Haucourt and held their men together under a very
severe fire of machine-guns and shrapnel. Both these officers
deserve great credit for the successful manner in which they
drew off their men after the action and eventually rejoined
headquarters.[148]

Poole himself was less than fulsome in his own praise for the men he
commanded. On 1 October 1914, in a somewhat ungracious entry under
his name in the battalion war diary, he commented, 'Discipline noticeably
worse than in South Africa. Probably due to socialistic ideas imbibed by
reservists.'

Haldane, in the meantime, was still struggling to carry out his orders to
form a rearguard to protect the retirement of 4 Division, even though
much of his brigade had either left the field already or was out of touch
with him altogether. His orders were to move his rearguard back in a
south-westerly direction by the valley between Caullery and Selvigny and
to take up the high ground behind the narrow gauge railway line south-
east of the Bois du Gard, about 2 miles south-east of Selvigny. A battery

of artillery under Major Short was attached to the rearguard to provide extra firepower should it be needed. It was not. The Germans made no attempt to pursue 4 Division and would only begin to move forward into Esnes, Haucourt and the other villages much later in the evening, after the withdrawal of 4 Division had been largely completed. Virtually the whole of 10 Brigade had been able to slip away without any serious pressure at all from the German infantry.

Haldane led his rearguard away from Selvigny at about 6pm. The route he had been given exposed the men to enemy fire and they came under a shower of shrapnel:

> As soon as we were clear of the area which was being shelled we marched along a track which was hidden from the view of the enemy and, crossing a light railway, came to what appeared to be the position we had been ordered to hold. It was now dark and rain had begun to fall and although I had doubts whether we had retired quite as far as was intended, I decided to halt. The map which had been issued to us did not, by the light of my electric torch, show the features of the ground at all clearly.[149]

Haldane was not happy with the orders he had been given by Snow for the retirement of his rearguard. Snow himself was unapologetic and felt that Haldane should have shown more initiative himself in carrying out these orders:

> In sending orders to General Haldane re his retirement from Haucourt, I remembered a sunken road or gully which I had ridden along in the morning and I told him to retire by this gully. He complained bitterly of the order afterwards as he said the gully was being heavily shelled. Of course it was within his power to act up to the spirit and not the letter of the order but I quote the incident to show how careful one should be in framing orders. I ought to have told him to retire on Selvigny and not given him a route. If I thought it best to call his attention to the sunken road I should have made it the substance of a message nothing to do with orders.[150]

Unsure as to whether he was in compliance with his orders, and concerned in case he was exposing the division to greater risk, Haldane decided to halt his rearward movement. He allotted bivouacs to the two battalions and sentries were mounted. He had witnessed during the course of the afternoon the actions of his subordinate commanders, who had taken upon themselves the decision as to when and how to retire. He was determined as far as possible not to do the same thing himself. He had not been given any information as to the whereabouts of the division and was not sure whether Snow was trying to get his men away from the battlefield quickly through a long night march or whether they might be taking up defensive positions nearby. If he pulled back even further from his present position he might be jeopardising the safety of the entire force.

In a note on the action at Haucourt written on 9 September, Haldane explained his reasons for remaining on the ground he held: 'My reason for remaining in this position was [that] although I felt there had been some mistake in my receiving no orders, I was loath to run the risk of compromising the retirement by withdrawing before I had definite orders to do so.' There is a clear echo between the words Haldane used to explain his actions on 26 August and his later note on retirements. A commendable determination not to give ground unnecessarily in case it compromised the safety of others took precedence over a willingness to assess the situation he was actually confronted with and to act on his own judgement. (In his later autobiography, published in 1948, Haldane provided a rather different explanation for his movements that night, conveying a sense of calmness not entirely apparent in his earlier accounts: 'I felt no anxiety at my rather isolated position for I felt sure that the Germans, like ourselves, would be tired and what I had seen of their cavalry had not impressed me.'[151])

Haldane himself collected some corn sheaves for a makeshift bed and slept under his waterproof coat. The men had no such coats and got thoroughly soaked. Somehow or other, probably through sheer exhaustion, Haldane and his men managed to sleep until about 3am. The rain had by now ceased and instead a faint mist hung over the dew-drenched fields. Haldane moved the men under his command to a new position further back. Captain Eric Campbell of the Seaforth Highlanders was sent off to Malincourt to see if there were any British troops there or any fresh orders for Haldane, as Major Daniell, who had earlier been dispatched to try to make contact with 4 Division, had not returned. At 5.45am Campbell returned with the grim news that the last of the British forces had left Malincourt at midnight, meaning that Haldane was on his own, several hours adrift from the main elements of the division, now heading south to Voyennes on the banks of the Somme, 4 miles to the west of Ham.

Snow had tried to help his men leave the battlefield in as good order as possible:

> I myself with my staff got on to the high ground east of Leheries and as long as the light lasted we managed, with the help of some gallopers from the artillery, to retrieve many wanderers. Unfortunately it got dark very suddenly owing to heavy rain commencing.[152]

Snow was hoping his retirement would not be detected by the enemy, although some of his men seemed to have other priorities:

> About midnight we arrived at Vendhuile. I felt sure that we had escaped unnoticed and I was anxious to keep our whereabouts secret. It was with some horror therefore that I saw the gunners setting fire to the stocks of oats, I suppose with a view to drying their clothes. The whole countryside was illuminated.[153]

Haldane in the meantime had rightly decided that his best course of action was to try to catch up with the rest of the division. He began a gruelling march, with no breaks for the men, en route to Gouy. The men with him had by this time exhausted their own supplies of rations and must have been dead on their feet. Eventually, however, Haldane and his party caught up with the division around Roisel, 10 miles from Gouy, Haldane having borrowed a staff car along the way from a hapless officer of the Army Service Corps.

Smith-Dorrien had passed some of the retreating parts of 4 Division during the night and was encouraging them to do everything possible to speed up their rate of progress. James Goodson, serving with 68 Battery of XIV Brigade, Royal Field Artillery, recalled the corps commander pointing to a bag of horseshoes on his wagon as he passed, telling him to 'throw that off'. It might well have been a false economy. A few days later Goodson had to turn loose a horse with worn-out shoes as he had no shoes to replace them with.

Although the day had ended badly for the Warwickshires and the Dublin Fusiliers, they could, in truth, regard their day's labour as having contributed significantly to the success of 4 Division at Le Cateau. They had stood their ground and repulsed the enemy whenever he had tried to advance against them. In doing so, they had defied all the odds. The German advance had been effectively blocked. The BEF was able now to withdraw to better positions, regroup and ultimately reinforce without facing any serious challenge from the Germans over the next few crucial days, when defeat stared the BEF in the face. The view of the *Official History* was clear and emphatic:

> ... the whole of Smith-Dorrien's troops had done what was thought to be impossible. With both flanks more or less in the air, II Corps had turned upon an enemy of at least twice their strength; had struck him hard, and had withdrawn, except on the right front of 5 Division, practically without interference, with neither flank enveloped, having suffered losses certainly severe, but considering the circumstances, by no means extravagant. The men looked upon themselves as victors. They had completely foiled the plan of the German commander.[154]

Von Kluck himself was led to believe that the main body of II Corps was pulling away to the south-west, in the general direction of Amiens, and set his compass in that direction for the following day. This made it possible for the tired but undefeated divisions of Smith-Dorrien's command to make good their retreat more or less unmolested on the 27th as they moved due south. It would be several more days before the British and German forces would confront each other again.

The losses for II Corps on 26 August were just under 8,000 men killed, wounded or missing. A total of 38 guns were lost. At 3,158 the losses in 4 Division were the highest of the three British divisions at Le Cateau. These losses were made worse because of the lack of its divisional field ambulance. Many of the wounded men had to be left where they lay. Heavy though these losses were, they were not as catastrophic as GHQ had at first feared. GHQ had in fact given up on II Corps altogether that night. Based on the briefings they had received from some British staff officers, who were themselves unaware of what was really going on, French liaison officers at GHQ began sending messages of doom and gloom to General Joffre at the French Headquarters. These messages brought grim news, confirming the demise of II Corps and the destruction of two entire divisions of the BEF. None of this was true.

Smith-Dorrien would later write, with some justification, that: 'It is undoubtedly a fact that after Le Cateau II Corps was no more seriously troubled during the ten days of retreat, except by mounted troops and mobile detachments who kept at a respectful distance.'

Once all the dust had settled, this view of Le Cateau as a successful engagement was also the verdict reached by Sir John French himself. In a celebrated dispatch to Kitchener on 7 September he wrote:

> I cannot close without putting on record my deep appreciation of the valuable services rendered by General Sir Horace Smith-Dorrien. I say without hesitation that the saving of the left wing of the army under my command on the morning of 26 August could never have been accomplished unless a commander of rare and unusual coolness, intrepidity and determination had been present to personally conduct the operation.[155]

In French's later memoirs he attempted to withdraw his original assessment of the battle of Le Cateau. The dispatch of 7 September was, he claimed, 'completed, of necessity, very hurriedly and before there had been time or opportunity to give thorough study to the reports ... by which alone the full details could be disclosed'. It is not clear to which reports he is referring. He would also exaggerate the extent of British losses at Le Cateau, claiming that they amounted to over 14,000 men and 80 guns. These figures were hugely overstated. He also asserted that the effect of the battle was to 'render the subsequent conduct of the retreat more difficult and arduous'. There is no basis for this claim whatsoever. In fact the opposite is true.

French would also falsely allege that the fate of II Corps was secured by the efforts of the cavalry division and the actions of Sordet's cavalry. Although late in the afternoon Sordet's men did provide valuable assistance, which protected the withdrawal of 4 Division, this cannot disguise the immense bravery and fighting power of the troops of 4 Division over the 12 hours the battle lasted and the contribution this made to the successful 'stopping blow' delivered by II Corps. Sordet's cavalry made the division's extraction easier than it might otherwise have been, but his contribution to the battle itself was not significant. The same is true of the British cavalry division. Despite the best efforts of the cavalry, they were in truth only bit-part players at Le Cateau. To put this into context, the cavalry corps as a whole suffered just 15 casualties throughout the whole of 26 August. Allenby himself, wisely, never sought to claim any credit for the successful outcome of the battle. Le Cateau was a battle fought entirely by infantry and artillery. The successes of both sides belonged to them and no one else.

The unpleasant spat between French and Smith-Dorrien reflected the very high levels of personal animosity between the two men and would continue to smoulder in the months after Le Cateau. The bad feeling generated would eventually lead to an even more cataclysmic row the following May, when French relieved Smith-Dorrien of his command of 2nd Army and sent him back to England under a cloud during the Second Battle of Ypres. French's later comments were a pathetic attempt to justify the way he had handled his long-standing personal rival in order to ensure that his own reputation prevailed at the expense of Smith-Dorrien's. This discreditable attempt failed altogether because it had no basis in fact and therefore collapsed at the first hurdle. On this occasion the verdict of history is clear: Smith-Dorrien's gamble at Le Cateau had worked. French himself made no contribution to this success and that is probably what irritated him the most.

The precise nature of the gamble taken by Smith-Dorrien is also clear from Snow's verdict on the day. Snow was never really clear about Smith-Dorrien's tactics for the battle and he was in truth profoundly in the dark about the real nature of the battle he was actually fighting:

> I had never been told, not even during that depressing interview at GHQ on the 24th, that the enemy were in overwhelming numbers and I was never made to understand that whatever the results of the battle, retreat was inevitable. This omission might have cost us dear ... I was convinced I was fighting a winning

action and indeed my left was advancing. Had I not stopped this advance and I did so because I heard we were to retire, my left would have been advancing at the very moment the enemy were in position to turn it and I should have been making his task easier. Thank goodness that night the enemy acted in an inconceivable manner and so our sins of omission were not visited on us, but I can never contemplate that night without a cold shiver down my back and if there are such things as lucky stars mine was functioning exceedingly well on my behalf that night. The worst mistake was not telling me that retreat was inevitable. Had I known that fact earlier I should have been able to have had the line of retreat reconnoitred and been able to have given more thought to how the retirement was to be carried out.

Looking back on the battle of Le Cateau, I have little to reproach myself with, but only one thing to congratulate myself about, and that one thing was the splendid behaviour of the men and the efficiency of the brigadiers, commanding officers and regimental officers. But when I have said that I have said it all. Very little, if anything, of what I did during the day had any effect on the result of the battle ...[156]

The result of the battle was, however, never really the issue. The battle could only end one way, given the numerical superiority of the Germans. It was instead the manner of the retreat of II Corps that was decided on 26 August. The likely rout became instead a largely untroubled retirement, allowing the BEF to regroup and fight another day.

For Elkington and Mainwaring 26 August had been a baptism of fire and by the evening of that day, despite all the gallantry and bravery of their men during the fighting at Haucourt, their immediate prospects looked pretty bleak as they made their bedraggled way from the field of conflict. Their battalions had split up into separate pieces. They were out of communication with brigade and division. They had no intelligence about the whereabouts of the enemy. They had no knowledge about the proper line of retreat. They had precious little ammunition or supplies of any kind. They were, at least, alive and uninjured. But the worst was still to come. The next day would effectively see their careers in the British Army come to an abrupt end.

Chapter 4

27 August: Surrender at St Quentin?

Hefty barbarians,
Roaring for war,
Are breaking upon us;
Clouds of their cavalry,
Waves of their infantry,
Mountains of guns.
Winged they are coming,
Plated and mailed,
Snorting their jargon.
Oh, to whom shall a song of battle be chanted?
                    Harold Monro, 'The Poets Are Waiting'

Although the retreat from St Quentin was not being vigorously pressed by the Germans, the general state of II Corps was by now a matter of real and growing concern at GHQ. The *Official History* summarised the harsh reality facing Smith-Dorrien's men on the night of 26/27 August:

Everywhere when the order to halt was given, the men dropped down on the road and were asleep almost before they reached the ground. The only precautions possible at the late hour were to push small piquets out a few hundred yards on each side of the road. Officers of the cavalry and artillery, themselves half dead with fatigue, had to rouse their men from a semi-comatose state to water and feed the horses and to rouse them once more to take the nose bags off, taking care lest they should fall asleep in the very act. And all of this had to be done in inky darkness under drizzling rain. Then the column got under way, drivers and troopers sleeping in their saddles, infantry staggering half asleep as they marched, every man stiff with cold and weak with hunger, but under the miraculous power of discipline, plodding on.[157]

This description closely matches the situation that Mainwaring faced that night as he arrived in Malincourt. His men had been on the move for three days without much rest and with little food or water. His priority was to put as much distance as possible between his men and the Germans. If he failed to do so, it was highly probable that their war would be over fairly rapidly. His options were not particularly attractive. They would have to overcome their exhaustion and fatigue and find the strength to continue their march to the south, or face almost certain death or imprisonment if they remained where they were. Having ordered his men to get some sleep in the barn at Malincourt at dusk, Mainwaring attempted to make contact with anyone in authority who could tell him what was going on and what he should do next. This was not easy. Smith–Dorrien had motored to St Quentin to confer with French, and the rest of his staff were by now many miles away to the south-east. The headquarters of 4 Division had already left the battlefield, heading initially towards Vendhuile, and as a result was out of communication with everyone else. Haldane and 10 Brigade Headquarters were still holding their rearguard position to the south-east of Selvigny, but they too were out of touch with everybody else in 4 Division and II Corps. In fact, no one had any idea where 10 Brigade was; they were certainly not where they were supposed to be as Haldane had delayed his retirement in order to try to establish what was happening.

Malincourt itself was a scene of total confusion as men from a number of units descended upon it in the darkness. General Snow explained the reasons for this confusion:

> It seems that 3 Division was given a route which took it through the east portion of Malincourt while 4 Division was given a route which took it through the west portion. This is never a safe proceeding with anything as small as a one inch map or smaller scale and the mix-up in Malincourt, not only of 3 and 4 Divisions but also of the 5th was appalling. Staff officers stood at the crossroads and asked each body of men or vehicles what they were and directed them accordingly.[158]

By degrees, the transport, artillery and some of the infantry of Snow's division were assembled into a column and began their eventual retirement to the south. Having been in touch with Divisional Headquarters for much of the battle itself, Mainwaring now found himself cut off from Snow. Ironically, and despite all of these difficulties, Mainwaring did manage, at last, to make contact with someone from the staff of 10 Brigade, a feat that had proved impossible throughout the fighting of the previous day:

> I met Major Daniell, acting brigade major of our brigade. He expressed great joy at seeing me, asked how many men I had, attached 60 of the Warwicks under a Special Reserve lieutenant to me and promised to send me orders. I pointed out the house we were in to him, put a sentry on the gate so that an orderly should find him and spent most of the time there myself. I did not dare lie down as all the rest did, as I had nobody on whom I could possibly depend to wake me up. This was my third night without one wink of sleep of any kind.

But Mainwaring never heard from Major Daniell again and did not receive any orders from him about the next stage of the retirement. Haldane had sent Daniell, the last remaining officer on his staff, to Malincourt in order to make contact with General Snow and obtain fresh orders about the retirement. Perhaps, in all the confusion, Major Daniell simply forgot about Mainwaring and his men, as they were not his priority. It is unclear what happened to Daniell that night. Haldane, for example, complained bitterly about the fact that Daniell did not return to him that evening either.

In truth, it is doubtful whether there was anyone in Malincourt who was in a position to give Mainwaring or Daniell any directions. The staff of 4 Division had long since departed. Mainwaring was simply left to fend for himself, like many others. After a couple of hours without orders, and in a state of rising anxiety about his own predicament, Mainwaring made another effort to find out what was going on and where he should try to take his men:

> After some two hours or less I again went to see if I could find why no orders had reached me. I found a cavalry regiment just

leaving, the last troops in the village, with the exception of ourselves. The cavalry colonel told me the retirement, his at least, was on two villages, L'Empire and Ronssoy, and left me. Consulting my map, I determined to march on the latter as being the more southerly, and waking the men myself, started somewhere a little before midnight.

The two small villages of L'Empire and Ronssoy stood on either side of a crossroads, and were in fact almost indistinguishable from each other. Getting there would involve a march of about 9 miles to the south-west of Malincourt in the general direction of 4 Division's retreat on Vendhuile. The main body of 4 Division was by now several hours ahead of Mainwaring and his party of stragglers. They would have a very tough job trying to catch up. Matters were not helped when Mainwaring failed to take the most direct route. He marched his men along the narrow country road to Villers Outreaux, where he proceeded almost due south to the village of Beaurevoir. But he had made a mistake and in the darkness took the wrong turning at a crossroads in the village. At 3am, realising he was not on the right road, and with no one else in sight, he decided to call a halt so the men could grab a bit more rest and he could get his bearings: 'I put the men into barns but again stayed up myself. The strain was cruel, but I could trust no one else.'

The pressure on Mainwaring was clearly intensifying. Physically as well as mentally, he was operating pretty well on his last reserves. To him and his men alike, the marching must have felt like an unfair punishment after everything they had been through. On top of the physical discomfort, Mainwaring must have been labouring under another, equally severe, stress as he had no idea whether his men were surrounded by the enemy on all sides; they might therefore be fired on or taken prisoner at any moment. Their retreat from Haucourt was certainly not in the nature of a leisurely stroll.

After a couple of hours' rest, Mainwaring led his men out of the village and on to the Roman road that had been the main axis for 5 Division's retreat from Le Cateau the day before. He was aiming for Estrees and then, if possible, for St Quentin, about 12 miles to the south via Joncourt and Levergies. A march of this duration must have been a daunting prospect for men who were already on their last legs. Shortly afterwards, in the bright and increasingly warm sunshine of what promised to be another glorious day, Mainwaring miraculously bumped into Elkington and his party, making their own way south from Ligny. From this moment onwards, their endeavour became a joint one and their fates were inextricably entwined.

Elkington had taken his party first towards Ligny, where he knew there were British forces, and then probably in the direction of Maretz before also heading south down the Roman road towards Estrees:

> I did not know in which direction we were supposed to retire. During the retirement in the dark it was impossible to keep the same men together for any length of time, there being so many stragglers and the men were continually falling out from exhaustion. About 2am I halted on the outskirts of a village and collected another 60 men of my battalion by 4am. I then continued my march. These men having had little to eat for 24 hours, my first thought was where to get them some food. I continued my march in the direction of St Quentin, which I knew to be a railway junction, and at about 8am I met Colonel Mainwaring with some men of his battalion and some of mine.

Private Hill, a member of Elkington's party, was finding the going hard:

> We came to a village jammed with retiring troops where an artillery officer bundled me off [the ammunition limber]. Fortunately some of my own regiment passed and seeing me lying in the road helped me along. My leg seemed easier and I was able to proceed at the pace my footsore companions were going. It was nightmare marching. Our party was now about 150 strong. Sleep was out of the question and food was begged from villagers.[159]

French civilians were doing all they could to ease the men's suffering. There were many good Samaritans along the roadside that day: women with jugs of water, baskets of fruit and even cups of strong black coffee for the soldiers to help keep them on their feet. Wine was also in plentiful supply, although this was less likely to help speed up the retreat or maintain march discipline. Officers and NCOs were ordered to make sure the men declined any offer of alcohol. Keeping the men moving was Elkington's primary concern and therefore finding food and water was essential. Having re-established contact with Mainwaring, Elkington made clear his destination was St Quentin, where he hoped there would be trains available to help the men get away from the enemy as quickly as possible: 'We continued our march together and managed in one village to obtain some loaves for the men which gave them a small piece each.'

Elkington estimated the size of the combined party at about 250 men, much bigger than the number suggested by Hill. Elkington's estimate would seem to be about right. Mainwaring thought that Elkington had about 100 men with him when they joined up on the road from Estrees. Having found each other, Mainwaring handed over command of his men to Elkington:

> We met Colonel Elkington with about 100 of his regiment and joined forces, he, being the senior, taking over the command. He told me he had already made up his mind to march on St Quentin. I very much doubted our ability to get them as far as St Quentin, but by dint of encouragement and pointing out that stragglers must become prisoners, and marching very slowly and with many halts we managed to reach that place between midday and 1pm.

The conditions experienced by the men on this morning were, by now, getting worse by the hour. Several days of fighting and marching, with little rest or food, was beginning to take an increasingly heavy toll, particularly on the Special Reservists. One of those soldiers moving down the road to St Quentin that morning was Sergeant John Collins, serving with the Royal Army Medical Corps attached to 7 Brigade:

> Some of them stood it better than others. In this blazing hot sun their feet had swollen inside their boots so they just could not bear to hobble along, so they took their boots off, cut them up in places, tied the laces together, hung them around their necks and then took off their putties and wound them around their feet and continued on the retreat that way.[160]

The retreating men of 4 Division trudging their way desperately towards St Quentin now bore little resemblance to the smartly turned out soldiers who had de-trained at Le Cateau only three short days before.

At St Quentin there was at least the possibility, as Elkington hoped, of some trains to get the men away, as well as the prospect of proper food and rest. It must have been this prospect, and this prospect alone, that kept the men moving. This part of the retreat from Le Cateau was now beginning to bear many of the hallmarks of defeat. The men were beginning to look less and less like soldiers in a professional army, and more like a ragged mass of dishevelled humanity. Unshaven, dirty, weary, their shoulders slumped and their uniforms either torn or missing, some without weapons, they did not inspire the same cheers and adulation among the French civilians now as they had done when they disembarked at Boulogne. There were other signs of defeat all around. There was little organisation and few supplies of food or ammunition for the men to stock up with. The road was filled with small mixed parties of men, not only from different battalions and brigades, but even from different divisions, with no one in overall command. Neither Mainwaring nor Elkington had any real idea who or what forces were in front or behind them, or indeed what was happening on their flanks. In any event, they were in no position to offer much resistance to the enemy. They were, in truth, at their lowest ebb since landing in France on 23 August.

By this time of the morning the road was full of stragglers like Elkington and Mainwaring's party. Most of the formed bodies had retired during the hours of darkness. According to Regimental Sergeant-Major Boreham of the 2nd Battalion, Royal Welch Fusiliers the road was 'full of small bodies of troops and of single men who had lost their units'.[161]

The sights they saw along this final stretch of the march to St Quentin were not likely to have lifted the morale of the men either. Smith-Dorrien, who had been trying to organise the retreat of his corps, had, on the evening of 26 August, driven along the very same road that Elkington and Mainwaring were now marching on. What he saw filled him with alarm as he witnessed:

a discreditable panic which occurred in an infantry column. At about 9.30 that evening when motoring from Estrees to St Quentin I saw for miles, by the light of my headlamp, boxes of ammunition thrown about on both sides of the road, and I actually found the commander and the column just clearing out of St Quentin empty. The OC told me that shots had been fired as he came along the road, he believed from Uhlans, and to save his men and horses he ordered all the ammunition to be thrown away and had galloped away and seemed very proud of it. From enquiries I made I came to the conclusion that it was extremely doubtful if there had been any enemy patrols there at all.[162]

Elkington likewise saw the ammunition boxes littering the roadside: 'Along the road we came across the discarded ammunition of some British artillery which extended for some miles; this did not have a cheering effect on our men who were tired and worn out.' In an effort to keep their spirits up, some of the soldiers coming down the road to St Quentin reached a very different and more cheerful conclusion about the abandoned ammunition. Gunner Bellow of I Battery, Royal Horse Artillery, attached to the cavalry division, recorded this observation on the morning of 27 August: 'We marched off at daybreak and went through the town of St Quentin. On the road we passed thousands of rounds of ammunition which had been abandoned by the enemy.'[163]

The ammunition was, of course, British. The Germans were still several miles to the north of St Quentin on the morning of 27 August and would not travel down this road for several more hours.

Captain Dunn of the 2nd Battalion, Royal Welch Fusiliers was marching with his battalion down the Roman road as dawn broke on the 27th: 'When it became light we saw more signs that we were part of a retreating army for we began to pass lorries that had broken down or run out of petrol and had been abandoned.' Captain Owens, with the 3rd Cavalry Field Ambulance, was hot on the heels of Captain Dunn: 'Infantry chaps were lying about all along the road side, absolutely dead beat. No greatcoats or anything, soaking wet and dead asleep.' The *Official History*, in a masterful understatement, also makes a particularly telling reference to the 'appearance of confusion which was completely absent on the [main] routes of those Divisions themselves'.

Elkington and Mainwaring were not, of course, on their own that morning. Earlier that day 1 and 2 Cavalry Brigades, as well as 19 Brigade and various battalions from 5 Division, had all passed through St Quentin, where they were fed and watered en route to Grand Seraucourt, a few miles to the south. At this time of the morning, progression through the town appeared to be fairly smooth. In the main, these were formed units that had left Le Cateau in reasonably good shape but other less well organised parties continued to stream down the Roman road towards St Quentin. The main line of retreat for both 5 Division and 19 Brigade was through the town and then on towards Ollezy, 4 miles to the east of Ham. At 5am the main body of 14 Brigade had marched into the town, received some food, was re-formed into its various constituent battalions and moved on. The remainder of the division came in later. Stragglers from both 3 and 4 Divisions, all mixed up together, and drifting eastwards rather than southwards as they should have been, were also heading for St Quentin. After a couple of hours' rest most of these men were back on their feet again and able to resume the retirement.

Behind these stragglers, however, and unbeknown to most of the exhausted infantry, a cavalry rearguard was desperately trying to protect the retiring troops from the attentions of the Germans. Tom Bridges was part of this rearguard:

> After two days of road work, I struck some of my own squadron still separated from the regiment, and feeling much better, got on a horse. I now collected all the stragglers I could find and for a time had a miscellaneous commando of about 150 horse composed chiefly of 5 Lancers and 4 Dragoon Guards. Eventually we regained our regiment and brigade and took part in several orthodox rearguard actions.[164]

In fact, the Germans were following the British at a relatively leisurely pace and made little attempt seriously to impede their progress towards St Quentin that morning. They were, after all, still licking their wounds from the previous day's fighting and were keeping a watchful distance. Elkington and Mainwaring, however, could not have known this crucial fact as they trooped wearily along the road to St Quentin under a blazing August sun, as no up-to-date intelligence was available to them. Nor were they aware of the presence of Tom Bridges and his cavalry rearguard. As far as they were concerned, there was nothing between them and the Germans.

By this time Bridges was in command of only two squadrons of cavalry and two companies of French Territorials who had been collected en route. The brigadier of 2 Cavalry Brigade had called Bridges and all his officers together early in the afternoon to brief them about the overall situation. It was not good, and a stiff upper lip seemed to be the order of the day: 'Our Brigadier said we were in a very tight corner, but must fight it out and die like gentlemen ... My orders were to hold the Germans off and retire through St Quentin at 6pm.'[165]

With these discouraging words ringing in his ears, Bridges made his own troop dispositions. He ordered the French troops to dig in on a rise north of the town and to remain there until 4pm. It was a good position, commanding a clear field of fire. Unfortunately, the Frenchmen decided on another, and altogether different, course of action. When Bridges checked on them shortly afterwards, they had already disappeared.

Meanwhile, Elkington and Mainwaring were approaching the town itself. Elkington had decided to halt his column just outside the town in order to assess the situation. Most of the men collapsed on the ground and fell asleep almost instantly. He observed two German cavalry patrols some distance away but they were keeping their distance and posed no immediate threat. He sent Mainwaring into the town in the hope that he might be able to make arrangements for getting the men food and drink, and perhaps find some trains that could take them away to safety. Taking a few men with him, Mainwaring duly headed off into St Quentin, where he had a surprise encounter with the commander of II Corps:

> Colonel Elkington sent me on to see what could be done, and I met General Smith-Dorrien in the town and told him the men were done. He told me it was a marvel that any of us had got away, that we had been up against four and a half to five German Army Corps and that he would give us a train to Noyon, if I could get one, and that if I could not he advised me to march some 5 miles further on the road to Ham and join 3 Division. [When] a member of his staff reminded him that it had marched from there, he said, 'There are some details there, you had better try and join them.' I said I doubted if our men could do it and that I would at all events try for a train first. I sent this information to Colonel Elkington, asking him to march to the station.

Smith-Dorrien had done all he could to try to arrange for some trains to take away his exhausted soldiers. The night before he had held a meeting with the Director of Railways in St Quentin, who had suggested that trains could be made available for this purpose provided the Quartermaster General at GHQ gave his permission. Unfortunately, GHQ had moved 30 miles away to Noyon on the evening of the 26th, but Smith-Dorrien, dogged in his pursuit of what he considered to be essential help for his battered corps, had driven to Noyon and secured agreement for these trains to be provided on the 27th. Implementing this agreement, however, would prove to be impossible, given the deteriorating conditions. The railway staff had fled and the trains were nowhere to be found.

The situation that confronted Mainwaring, Elkington and Smith-Dorrien in St Quentin that day was grim and deeply depressing. The men who had managed to reach the town were literally at the limits of their physical endurance. Harold Gibb, a chaplain attached to GHQ, passed through the town at about midday and found men 'scattered about the town, propped up against the walls of houses, sleeping on pavements, or lying in gutters, numbed by fatigue and lack of sleep'.[166] Captain Arthur Osburn RAMC, the Medical Officer serving with 4 Dragoon Guards, witnessed similar scenes:

> The whole square was thronged with British infantrymen standing in groups or wandering about in an aimless fashion, most of them without either packs or rifles. Scores had gone to sleep sitting on the pavement, their backs against the fronts of the shops. Many exhausted lay at full length on the pavement. Some few, obviously intoxicated, wandered about firing in the air at real or imaginary German aeroplanes. The great majority were not only without their arms but had apparently either lost or thrown away their belts, water bottles and other equipment.[167]

Osburn estimated that there were several hundred soldiers milling about in the square but he could see very few officers. No one seemed to be in command and it appeared that the majority of the soldiers were in no fit state to offer very much effective resistance to the enemy.

Sergeant John Collins was also in St Quentin at about the same time. He recalled: 'When we got to St Quentin, all over the square and in the roads were infantrymen lying fast asleep, absolutely whacked to the world, stragglers from the battle of Le Cateau the day before.'[168] Another man who managed to reach St Quentin that morning was Corporal William Holbrooke of the 4th Battalion, Royal Fusiliers, 3 Division: 'We halted at St Quentin. They were in a bad way then – some were sitting on the side of the road crying.'[169] Certainly the men desperately needed rest and something to eat and drink. Some of the battalions in St Quentin took matters into their own hands. Major Geiger of the 2nd Battalion, Royal Welch Fusiliers, for example, described how he found food for his men:

> We were feeling pretty hungry and I was sitting opposite a grocer's shop. That led to the suggestion to the CO that he ration the battalion and so he bought up the shop. The epicier protested but he accepted our requisition. Potted meats, jams, biscuits, chocolate and anything that could be eaten ...[170]

According to Tom Bridges, he sent Lieutenant Harrison, one of his subalterns, to go into St Quentin in order to check that the infantry were progressing satisfactorily through the town. Harrison, however, brought back some very unwelcome news: 'On his return he reported the place swarming with stragglers, he could find no officers and the men were going into the houses and lying down to sleep.'[171]

In truth, staff officers had, since the early hours of the morning, been attempting to sort out the mess in the town square and get the soldiers back on their feet and reunited with their units. They erected in the square a large blackboard indicating which roads troops from the various divisions should take on their way out of the town. As the day wore on, most of the better organised units left the town, leaving behind those who were without leadership and lacked the motivation to carry on without it.

Elkington, having received his own progress report from Mainwaring, marched his command into the town and proceeded immediately to the railway station, hoping to get on board the waiting trains. He arrived there at about 2pm. It soon became apparent that there was no possibility of any trains leaving the station that day, as all the railway staff had already vanished, fearing for their lives. The two colonels resolved that they would make an effort to reach Ham on foot. Before they could do this, the men would need to rest before embarking on another exhausting march on the road south. Their men were in a state of collapse. To make matters worse, the sun was by now high in the sky, pouring a remorseless and unforgiving heat into the dusty streets of the town. Parched and hunger-stricken, the men desperately needed food, water and rest.

At this crucial point in the day General Hobbs, the Deputy Adjutant and Quartermaster-General at I Corps, arrived in the station forecourt in a motor car. Precisely what he was doing there is not clear, as I Corps had not retired through St Quentin that day and Haig's headquarters lay many miles away to the east. But Hobbs made what would prove to be a uniquely unhelpful intervention. He suggested to Elkington and Mainwaring that they should both go to see the town mayor, who might be able to arrange a train for the men or at the very least some food for them. Elkington immediately dispatched Mainwaring to visit the Mairie and see what he could fix up. However, the Mayor of St Quentin, Arthur Gibert, had only taken over this office the day before, and had been somewhat reluctant to take on such high civic office. The former mayor and his deputy had both fled the town together on the 26th for fear they would be executed by the Germans as both men originated from Alsace and Lorraine, disputed French territories that had been occupied by the Germans since the Franco-Prussian War of 1870. According to the transcripts of council meetings at that time, General French had warned the council on the 26th, as he was making good his own exit from the town, that the Germans were systematically shooting civic officials who came from these two Departments and that they had therefore better flee immediately. Monsieur Gibert, one of the few remaining town councillors, had been suddenly volunteered by his colleagues for the job. Not surprisingly, there were no other candidates for the vacancy.

Mainwaring, dead on his feet, was dispatched back up the steep hill to the Mairie, which was situated in the troop-filled town square, about three-quarters of a mile from the railway station. On arrival he found the mayor in an excitable mood:

> The Mayor told me there was no chance whatever of a train but that he would send us some food, which I asked him to expedite. At this moment a breathless messenger handed a note

to the mayor, who on reading it became very excited, throwing up his hands and exclaiming it was the end, all was lost. The room was full of excited Frenchmen so I told my interpreter to tell me exactly what was in the note.

It was grim news. The note informed the mayor that the town was completely surrounded by the Germans and that it was impossible for anyone to leave: 'I was leaving the room when the mayor caught sight of me and said, "Ah! Your troops will spoil all. The Germans will shell the town now and the women and children will be killed" or words to that effect.' Mainwaring told the mayor he would do nothing to jeopardise the safety of civilians: 'I said you need not fear; if we cannot get our men away, we will not fight in the town. I must go and see my commanding officer.'

Mainwaring was in no doubt that the mayor's information concerning the proximity of the Germans was correct: 'We [presumably a reference to Elkington] neither of us doubted the authenticity of the mayor's statement for we had ourselves seen shells bursting only some 7 or 8 miles north of St Quentin, more than three hours previously.' It was not unreasonable for Mainwaring to assume that St Quentin was surrounded. He had no hard and fast information about the whereabouts of the enemy, but everything he had seen on the dismal retreat from Haucourt, and the lack of any obvious organisation or command, would have entitled him to assume the worst. After all, this was in line with much of what had happened so far to him and his battalion since they had landed in France only four days previously. The apparent threat to the French civilians in St Quentin would now dominate the thoughts and actions of both Elkington and Mainwaring over the next few crucial hours. Mainwaring in particular became convinced he had an overriding duty to protect the local inhabitants from the risk of being drawn into the fighting and having their homes destroyed or their lives put at risk. And in the absence of any information to the contrary, these were not unreasonable or unworthy factors for either colonel to take into account. Elkington would later claim, however, that he was much more sceptical about the imminent danger posed to the town by the Germans, although there is no evidence indicating that he ever expressed these doubts to anyone at the time. His behaviour at the critical moments is certainly consistent with him taking the same view as Mainwaring.

Mainwaring hurried back down the hill to the railway station to discuss the rapidly deteriorating situation with Elkington. Both agreed on the direness of their predicament. A decision needed to be taken. Should they stay and fight it out at the railway station, or should they try to get out of the town before the Germans arrived and fight them on better ground with less risk of collateral damage? Alternatively, should they throw in the towel and give up the fight altogether, as they were hardly well placed to mount a serious defence? Many of their men had neither the equipment nor the necessary strength to fight. But they also knew that if they gave up, their men would almost certainly be taken prisoner. These were the stark and difficult choices that confronted them. Conveying the gravity of the situation to the men would pose further problems. They had persuaded them to keep going on the promise of trains and food when they reached St Quentin. Neither now looked likely. The prospect of a further long, hot and difficult march or of a final, last-ditch stand would hardly be welcome news. It would test both the men's discipline and their resilience to the very limits.

Up to this moment, there is a remarkable similarity between Elkington's and Mainwaring's accounts of the retreat from Haucourt, but it is at this critical juncture that their respective versions of events began to diverge markedly. According to Elkington, both men agreed that they must not endanger the safety of the inhabitants by fighting inside the town. Elkington thought the mayor should calm down:

> I told him [Mainwaring] to go to pacify the Maire and tell him I would not fight in the town but our men must have rest and food. There was never the slightest intention in either of our minds to surrender to anyone nor did we do so. We fully intended to leave St Quentin and continue our march on Noyon directly the men were rested. If surprised by the Germans, my intention was to fight at the back of the station and not in the streets so as to save unnecessary slaughter of the women and children of whom the town was full.

This account reveals what was in Elkington's mind. His men needed time to recover their strength before they could resume their march out of the town. But he was clear they would defend themselves if they were attacked and would do so in a way that would minimise the risk of civilian casualties.

Mainwaring, however, records a completely different account of their consultation at the railway station:

> Colonel Elkington agreed that we must not endanger the safety
> of the inhabitants by fighting in the town. I addressed the men
> and he addressed his. I told mine that I would lead them out
> then and there and try to get to Noyon, a distance of 25 miles,
> if they would make the attempt BUT NOT ONE MAN OFFERED TO
> COME. The fact is that the men could do no more for the time
> being. Their limit of endurance was reached. I considered it my
> duty to protect these men who so nobly had done theirs. He
> [Elkington] therefore ordered me to surrender and while I was
> doing so he disarmed the men, putting their rifles and
> ammunition in one railway shed and them in another.

This does not seem to ring true. If a decision had in fact been taken to surrender at this point, it is rather surprising that Elkington, the senior of the two colonels and in overall command, did not himself seek to conduct the negotiations with the mayor.

Elkington did speak to his men in the station forecourt as Mainwaring reported, and it is clear that he was equally unable to spark any enthusiasm for the march to Noyon. Not a single soldier volunteered to continue the march. Elkington knew the men were physically and mentally exhausted. But he would later flatly contradict Mainwaring's suggestion that he ordered him to surrender his men to the Maire. He conceded that the rifles and ammunition were stored in a separate shed to where the men were accommodated, but this, he insisted, was in order to ensure the men could get some proper rest and some food. There was no suggestion of 'disarming' the men. The rifles could be 'easily got in the case of need', he claimed. It was undoubtedly a strange thing for Elkington to have put his men in one shed and their arms and ammunition in another, and his explanation is not particularly convincing, given the fact he knew the Germans were not that far behind them. Such an arrangement hardly lent itself to the possibility of mounting a rapid defence if the Germans suddenly arrived. He may have been concerned that the men were not in a fit state to be in possession of their weapons, although there is no direct evidence of drunkenness or other threats to discipline. But in Elkington's defence, at this moment in time there was no one for him to surrender his men to anyway. The Germans had not yet arrived in the town and neither had any German officer invited him to lay down his arms. At this time the notion of surrender was, in his view, simply a theoretical concept.

With the benefit of hindsight, all this can be seen as the actions of two very tired commanders struggling to make rational decisions against an extremely challenging backdrop. Their behaviour may well be difficult to rationalise, but in the context of what was happening in the town at the time, it is possible to take a less critical view of their decisions.

There was a darker mood among the men, who knew they were in a bad situation and that it was getting worse by the hour. Private Hill, who was with the Royal Warwickshires at the railway station, remembered how he felt at this time: 'Reaching St Quentin, we had great hopes of rest, but were told that we were surrounded. We lay down to die through sheer weariness... .'[172]

Mainwaring, however, was now acting under a different impulse. He made his way once more back up the hill to speak to the mayor again. The journey made a powerful impression on him. The sights and sounds along the way made him more and more convinced that there was only one course of action open to him:

> As I rode back to the Mairie I saw terrified women dragging their children indoors and everyone putting up their shutters. Everyone but ourselves and a few stragglers had fled and as I rode up my brain became obsessed with the one idea that our duty was to save nameless horrors overtaking these poor defenceless creatures. It was Thursday afternoon. I had not slept since Monday morning I had seen villages burning and others shelled. I could think of nothing else and that is the whole truth.

Mainwaring's account reveals the turmoil of an officer worn down with exhaustion and wracked with doubt about the wisdom of continuing the fight against a rampant enemy who had shown no mercy in his relentless advance into France. But he was not correct in saying that most of the British soldiers had by now left the town. There were still several hundred soldiers in and around the square.

When he got to the Mairie in the town square, he found the mayor and his advisers still fearing a final, terrible onslaught from the Germans. Mainwaring offered to surrender the men under his and Elkington's command. The town officials then drew up a surrender document and Mainwaring signed it, adding some details about the number of men under his command and the names of the officers. He made clear it would be an unconditional surrender, as his men were unable to march away:

> I felt if I argued as to conditions, it might leave an opening for the Germans to shell the town and kill the civilian population and I then felt my duty was to make no attempt at terms. Prostrated with mental and physical exhaustion, I wrote those words convinced I was doing my duty and a noble act.

The plan seemed to be for the mayor, rather than Mainwaring or Elkington, to present the surrender document to the Germans as they advanced into the town, as the paper Mainwaring had signed remained in the possession of Maire Gibert throughout. With the benefit of hindsight, this might not have been the best route to follow as it provided no obvious way of ensuring the town did not come under enemy bombardment – the very objective of the whole surrender exercise. Nor would it have given the Germans much genuine comfort about the real intentions of any remaining British units in the town. The intention to surrender could not in truth be easily communicated through or by an intermediary – it could only come first-hand from the troops themselves.

Elkington claimed to be completely unaware that a surrender document had been signed. His version of events is markedly different from Mainwaring's in almost every important respect:

> Colonel Mainwaring proceeded to the mayor with an interpreter and signed a paper to the mayor. This paper I never saw till the trial and did not know till then how it was worded. I am sure when [he] signed it he did so under great mental and physical strain and did not realise the consequences. I thought at the time the mayor was exaggerating the situation.

Elkington is quite clear that he had not ordered Mainwaring to sign a surrender document, in fact quite the opposite. However, his comments are equivocal about whether or not at some point in the afternoon he became aware that a surrender had indeed been concluded. There is no direct evidence that he ever tried to counter any suggestion that his men would surrender. There is plenty of evidence to confirm that his men were in no doubt their officers had decided to surrender, as became quite plain when Bridges and his fellow officers tried to persuade the men to fall in and resume the retreat – an event directly witnessed by both Elkington and Mainwaring.

By the middle of the afternoon it was clear to Bridges that most of the stragglers from the day before had cleared the area and that only the occasional lame duck was still coming down the Le Cateau road. It was time for him to think about moving his rearguard through and beyond the town. He therefore left some of his men and their machine-guns to hold the bridge over the river to the north while he came into St Quentin to make an assessment of the situation in the town. Time was still on the side of the British forces. The Germans were in no hurry to reach St Quentin. According to Bridges:

> The Germans were slow in coming on. During the afternoon a large grey car loaded with ladies came up on to a hill nearby and [they] had a good look round. The car was so like a staff Benz that we thought the sex of the ladies doubtful. We sent a patrol to investigate but [the car] quickly turned and was gone.[173]

When Bridges arrived in the town, it was clear that someone needed to get a firm grip on the situation:

> There were two or three hundred men lying about in the Place and the few officers with them, try as they would, could not get a kick out of them. Worse, Harrison now reported that the remains of two battalions had piled arms in the railway station and that their commanding officers had given a written assurance to the Maire that they would surrender and fight no more, in order to save the town from bombardment.[174]

A decisive moment had been reached in this extraordinary day. Into the chaos had stepped a fresh and determined character who, unlike most of the others around him, was not suffering in the same way from the physical and mental tribulations of the last few days. Bridges had a much clearer appreciation of the tactical situation and knew more about the whereabouts of the enemy than anyone else. He also knew there was time to get these men safely out of the town and back into the fight at some point in the future, and he was not prepared to see them surrender unnecessarily. His first priority was to seize possession of the surrender document and then to get the exhausted men ready to march out of the town towards Ham and safety.

Bridges conducted his delicate negotiations with the two colonels through an intermediary, Lieutenant Harrison. Bridges knew Elkington personally and had met Mainwaring on previous occasions, although both officers were of course senior to him in rank. When Harrison rode into the station forecourt, a stormy meeting ensued.

As the weary soldiers gathered around him, Harrison told them that St Quentin was protected by a cavalry rearguard and that they must hurry up and get out while they could. They refused to be persuaded. Accounts differ about what happened next. In Mainwaring's account of the meeting, it is implicit that he told the young cavalry officer that a surrender had already been decided upon and that it was too late to withdraw:

> At about 4pm a cavalry subaltern rode into the station yard calling the men to turn out and follow him. They utterly refused to. *I explained the situation.* He abused them and left.

According to Bridges' account, the men organised a meeting and 'refused to march on the ground that they had already surrendered and would only come away if a train was sent to take them'.[175]

Arthur Osburn's recollections are more graphic but probably less reliable, although they are corroborated in part by Mainwaring. Osburn thought it was Bridges himself who addressed the throng of soldiery in the station forecourt. He could not hear what he said, but noted that whatever it was, it did not inspire a very warm response from those gathered around him. He recalled, '[Bridges] harangued this disorganised mob, after which one of the soldiers had shouted, "our old man has surrendered to the Germans and we'll stick to him. We don't want any bloody cavalry interfering", whereupon he pointed his rifle at Bridges. I began to wonder whether Bridges would be shot if he continued his harangue at the railway station.'[176]

The remark that a rifle was aimed at the cavalry officer addressing the crowd may be an exaggeration, as according to all other accounts the men had already been disarmed. Elkington was washing when Harrison rode into the station yard:

> I heard a noise in the station yard. Colonel Mainwaring rushed out and I followed. We found a cavalry officer addressing the men. They were taking no notice of him. Colonel Mainwaring at once spoke to the men and said if they remained with him he would see them through. I saw the situation had changed and that all was clear. I urged the men to fall in and come out with me but they would not.

Three things are striking in this version of events. First, Elkington and Mainwaring were now publicly at odds with each other. Secondly, it is clear that Elkington had by now lost all control over what was left of his battalion, as not a single soldier of the Warwickshires was prepared to follow him. Thirdly, it must by now have been apparent to Elkington that Mainwaring had indeed agreed to surrender his force to the Germans. This is the only logical conclusion from the 'explanation' referred to in Mainwaring's own account of the meeting, and the outcome of the initial encounter with Harrison in the station yard.

From this point onwards Elkington and Mainwaring were to take different paths. Elkington made the decision that it was time for him to leave St Quentin and to try to rejoin his battalion:

> As I saw the danger was passed and they could get out when they chose, I left the yard at about 5.30pm as I was anxious to get on and collect more stragglers. I found a deserted horse on the square and some discarded British saddlery. I saddled the horse and rode out of St Quentin exactly at 6pm. On the way I collected a large number of stragglers from different battalions and marched towards Noyon.

It is odd, to say the least, that Elkington would choose to leave all his men behind him like this and slip away quietly without apparently letting anyone know. Mainwaring, for one, seems to have been unaware of his departure. If it was clear that they could in fact 'get out when they chose', why would he not leave with his men, who were, after all, his primary responsibility? What had happened to the brave, decisive commander of the day before? His desire to round up men from other battalions and take them to safety lacks plausibility given the fact that he had left behind him in the station yard over 150 of his own men. A less favourable interpretation might suggest another motive: self-survival. Elkington must by now have realised that after Mainwaring's attempted surrender he was in an extremely difficult position. It could perhaps be inferred from his strange behaviour that he wanted no part of the responsibility for leading his men into captivity as prisoners of war, or worse, into prison at the hands of a court martial.

Elkington claimed that he left St Quentin in the company of a major. However, he never identified his companion and it seems certain from all the various accounts provided by officers of the Royal Warwickshires that this unidentified major was not from Elkington's battalion.

By now Mainwaring was on his own at the station. Bridges was determined to try once more to persuade him to leave with his men. This time he dispatched Captain Sewell of the 4th Dragoon Guards to reason with the men. By this time, it must have begun to dawn on those waiting at the station that the Germans were not pressing forward into the town. There were no sounds of shelling or any small arms fire. Everything was quiet. Maybe there was the possibility of slipping away after all.

Bridges decided to make his position clear and unambiguous:

> I sent an ultimatum giving them half an hour's grace, during which time some carts would be provided for those who really could not walk, but letting them know that I would leave no British soldier alive in St Quentin. Upon this they emerged from the station and gave no more trouble.[177]

This time Mainwaring responded more positively: 'Later on a cavalry captain arrived, accompanied by the same subaltern. He told me he could guide us out, when I at once said every man would thankfully come. By now I was in command as Colonel Elkington had left.' It had evidently dawned on Mainwaring that the situation he was confronting had fundamentally changed: 'As time passed on, it became clear that something had delayed the German advance and I began to pray for darkness.'

Another concern also entered his mind: the existence of the surrender document. Mainwaring not surprisingly wanted it back. He was undoubtedly aware that the document presented a problem for him. Given the conversations in the station yard and Bridges' ultimatum, there could have been no doubt in his mind that his decision to sign the surrender document lay absolutely at the centre of any future controversy surrounding his and Elkington's conduct. Unfortunately for him, others also wanted to take possession of the incriminating evidence. Bridges was fully aware of the importance of this paper and its significance in any possible disciplinary proceedings, and had resolved to get it back from the mayor as quickly as possible. Mainwaring reported:

> I said I must get the paper back from the mayor. The cavalry officers said they meant to have that. I said I didn't mind who had it as long as it was recovered. The cavalry subaltern accompanied me to the Mairie and, pushing on in front, demanded the paper. I was too proud to argue with him for possession of it as I was still upheld with the conviction that I had done my duty. They took it and sent it to their General.

The sense conveyed in this dispirited account is that of a man who was now broken not just physically but in spirit as well. Here was a lieutenant-colonel bowing to the superior authority of a second lieutenant 30 years his junior. Any vestige of command had entirely deserted him. It is not clear to whom the surrender document was sent, but it probably worked its way up the chain of command. It would have explosive consequences for Elkington and Mainwaring.

Mainwaring returned to the railway station empty handed and crestfallen. He told the men that the surrender was off because the Germans were not about to enter the town after all. He urged the men to get ready to leave the town with him, and they would try to rejoin the rest of the battalion, wherever it was. After a few minutes the men fell in, collected their arms and ammunition and filled up their water bottles as they prepared to resume their retreat. Carts and wagons were being requisitioned to carry away those who could not walk. At 9pm they marched into the town square and halted, awaiting further orders. Bridges had asked Osburn to count all the stragglers left in the town and get them sorted into groups of four. Osburn counted over 200 men of the Dublin Fusiliers and Royal Warwickshires. Mainwaring was, by his own account, in a bad way: 'This was my fourth night without sleep, and twice I fell down when standing up.' Osburn believed that Mainwaring was on his last legs, describing him as:

> looking very pale, entirely dazed, had no Sam Browne belt and leaning heavily on his stick, apparently so exhausted with fatigue and heat that he could scarcely have known what he was doing. Some of his men called to him encouraging words, affectionate and familiar, but not meant insolently – such as 'Buck up sir! Cheer up daddy! Now we shan't be long! We are all going back to Hang-le-tear![178]

Having assembled the troops at the station into some kind of order, Bridges' next priority was to re-establish control over the troops in the town square. Here there would be no need to threaten the execution of those who disobeyed orders. The first priority was to get the men back on their feet, after which it should be possible to get them marching again. Music held the key. One of the shops in the square was a toy shop, and so far it had escaped the attention of the starving and thirsty soldiers. Bridges had a simple but brilliant idea:

> The men in the square were so jaded it was pathetic to see them. If only one had a band, I thought! There was a toy shop handy which provided my trumpeter and myself with a tin whistle and a drum and we marched round and round the fountain where the men were lying like the dead, playing 'The British Grenadiers' and 'Tipperary' and beating the drum like mad. They sat up and began to laugh and even to cheer. I stopped playing and made them a short exhortation and told them I was going to take them back to their regiments. They began to stand up and fall in.[179]

Bridges' timely arrival into St Quentin had, without any doubt whatsoever, saved the day and prevented an unnecessary surrender. Were it not for his efforts and those of his junior officers, several hundred British soldiers would have been captured by the Germans and made prisoners of war. His intervention would, however, have darker consequences for Mainwaring and Elkington.

At about 10pm the remnants of a dozen or more regiments started to leave the town. The night air was heavy with mist and the men felt their way forward cautiously. The convoy was making its way south-west towards Ham. Progress was slow, partly because of the mist but also because of the condition of the men. The wagons that had been requisitioned for the wounded and exhausted soldiers were quickly filled up. These wagons also slowed the rate of progress. Mainwaring described the scene:

> We moved very slowly, with a cavalry escort, and at about 2am
> we halted at a farm and village called Roupy. Here the cavalry
> left us and after blocking the road by putting the wagons across
> it, and posting piquets on it, I lay down and slept till dawn, the
> first sleep I have been able to get since Monday morning.

The tiny village of Roupy was on the main road from St Quentin to Ham. The going was painfully slow, as Mainwaring acknowledged – it took his party over 4 hours to travel just over 10 miles. The headquarters of his battalion, in the meantime, had moved down from Haucourt to Voyennes, a further 10 miles away but Mainwaring was at least heading in the right direction. He and his party would march all day on the 28th, finally reaching Noyon, another 20 miles away to the south. Here he and his men finally found the elusive trains they had long searched for and were taken to Compiegne. It would be several days yet before Mainwaring would meet up with the rest of his battalion and resume command. His personal account of this final section of the long and difficult retreat from Le Cateau had by this point become an entirely self-justificatory monologue. As day broke at Roupy, for example, Mainwaring recorded the views he claimed were expressed by two of the escorting cavalry officers: 'Soon after daybreak the cavalry rejoined us and escorted us some way until, telling us to make for St Sulpice, they left us. I must say here that before the two officers withdrew both of them shook hands with me and said I had done everything a man could do.'

Elkington meanwhile was also heading towards Voyennes. Although there is no clear evidence, it is highly likely that he would have taken pretty much the same route as Mainwaring, as this was the main road out of St Quentin to the south-west. The war diary of the 1st Battalion, Royal Warwickshires records that Elkington, along with Major Christie and about 280 other men, rejoined the battalion around Voyennes/Bussy the following day. On that day Elkington resumed command of his battalion and rejoined the brigade, which would continue the general retreat until 5 September and the beginning of the Battle of the Marne. It was a largely uneventful time for both the division and the brigade. Because they were so few in number, the Dublin Fusiliers and the Warwickshires had been merged into a composite battalion pending the return of their missing men. They were ordered to help repel the German cavalry and artillery attack at Nery on 1 September but arrived after the fighting had ended. It would be their only brush with combat action.

While the retreat continued, time was running out for both Elkington and Mainwaring. It is not clear what happened to the surrender document. It was clearly passed up the chain of command, but which officer made the final decision to summon a court martial and why this course of action was preferred over other, less visible forms of disciplinary action is still a matter of conjecture. The most probable source of the arrest order was GHQ. Dirty washing is often best dealt with in private, but in this case there was a wider issue of morale and reputation to deal with, as the attempted surrender at St Quentin clearly reflected the 'wrong' image of the retreat from Mons, which was being widely represented as an heroic success against overwhelming odds.

Rather revealingly, Haldane admitted that on the day of Elkington's arrest he was visited by Sir Archibald Murray, French's Chief of Staff at GHQ. Although he makes no mention of it in his memoirs, it would be very strange if the arrest order had not also been discussed by the two men. Haldane certainly felt strongly about the issue of morale in his brigade. On the day of Elkington's arrest he wrote, 'I do not think that a single individual of the brigade had lost that innate feeling of superiority over the foe and the utter impossibility of being vanquished by him.'

Whether this rosy view extended in Haldane's mind to Elkington and Mainwaring is unclear.

Allenby, the officer commanding the cavalry division, made no reference to the incident at St Quentin and would not have been part of the decision-making process. It is much more likely that the paper eventually reached GHQ and it was here that the decision to prosecute the two colonels was taken. The fact that the men under the command of Elkington and Mainwaring were clearly not in contact with the enemy at the time of the attempted surrender must have been a strong factor in the decision to set up a court martial, while the heroic last-ditch stands made by other battalions caught up in the retreat, like the Gordon Highlanders and the Cheshires, would only have served to highlight the contrast between what happened at St Quentin and elsewhere since the fighting had erupted at Mons on 23 August. General Snow recorded in his diary that he was ordered to place Elkington and Mainwaring under arrest. Only his corps commander or GHQ could have issued him with such an order.

The war diary of 10 Brigade[180] records that Elkington was placed under arrest at 11.30am on the morning of Saturday, 5 September, as the battalion was taking a break during another long route march which had started at dawn from Brie-Compt-Robert to Chevry. At this point Major Poole, who had only just been reunited with his regiment, together with over 400 other men, was given temporary command of the battalion. On the same day Colonel Churcher, Haldane's particular *bête noire*, was also relieved of his command and sent back to England. His misdemeanours are not recorded. Presumably Mainwaring was arrested at the same time as Elkington – this is explicit in General Snow's account of events, although the war diaries of both the brigade and the battalion are silent on the matter. It was only two days later, when the battalion had moved forward to a position south-west of Crecy, that the brigade war diary confirmed that the Dublin Fusiliers had a new commanding officer, Captain Frankland.

Chapter 5

12 September: Court Martial

Oh! We, who have known shame, we have found release there,
Where there's no ill, no grief, but sleep has mending,
Naught broken save this body, lost but breath;
Nothing to shake the laughing heart's long peace there
But only agony, and that has ending;
And the worst friend and enemy is but death.

Rupert Brooke, 'Peace'

On Saturday, 12 September, exactly one week after Elkington's arrest, Mainwaring and Elkington stood trial late in the afternoon before a court martial at Chouy, a small village about 10 miles south-east of Villers-Cotteret. They faced two charges. The first was cowardice, perhaps the most reprehensible offence under military law. If they were found guilty of this charge, they faced possible death by firing squad. The second, less serious, charge was dishonourable conduct, having behaved in a scandalous manner unbecoming the character of an officer and a gentleman in that they 'At St Quentin, on 27th August 1914, during a retirement following on an engagement at Ligny, without due cause, agreed together to surrender themselves and the troops under their respective command.' The charge of dishonourable conduct did not carry a death sentence. Instead, both men faced being cashiered from the army.

The president of the court martial was Brigadier-General Aylmer Hunter Weston, commander of 11 Brigade. A soldier of the old school, Hunter Weston had attended the Staff College at roughly the same time as many of the more senior commanders of the BEF, but his career had developed on a slightly flatter trajectory. He was perfectly happy to be in command of a brigade, where he displayed a deep concern for the welfare of his troops; in the years before war broke out, he had invested considerable personal energy into their training and overall readiness. He was undoubtedly a brave leader. Several times during the fighting on

26 August, for example, he had led his men, literally, from the front. In a letter home to his wife he recounted how:

> On three occasions [the 1st Battalion, Hampshires] retired from their positions, but on each occasion, by personally leading them forward and explaining to the young soldiers that it was essential that they held this position, we were able to maintain the position without undue cost.[181]

Under his command 11 Brigade had earned a well–deserved reputation as one of the most aggressive units in the BEF – a trait that was clearly on display during the advance to the Aisne in September, where the brigade was in the very forefront of the fighting. His notion of command was, however, a rather unusual one. He largely confined himself to organisational matters, and once battle had commenced he generally considered his work was done – it was then simply a matter of waiting for the dust to settle. This sometimes resulted in him having time to pursue his favourite leisure activities while his men were engaged in combat. In his diary entry for 28 October 1914, for example, he and his brigade staff took the opportunity to shoot game while his soldiers were fighting nearby. According to Hunter Weston:

> The final bag was 6 pheasants, 7 rabbits and 3 hares. We should have done better if it had not been for the *garde forestier* who saved many rabbits' lives by shouting 'lapin' whenever he saw one and setting off in hot pursuit. The shoot was made more interesting by the Germans who were shelling the Chateau de la Hutte only 150 yards away from one of the stands with extraordinary accuracy. On the E edge of the wood we could hear German shells bursting and our rifle fire; to the N we heard our 60 pounders and to the S a brigade of 18 pounders was firing continuously. Aeroplanes of both sides were being shot at all the time over our heads and siege howitzers were doing steady work in the west end of the wood.[182]

There is more than a hint of caricature about the scene depicted in this strangely comic prose. Shooting was certainly a popular sport among officers, although it would have been less common to organise a game shoot during a battle. Hunter Weston was clearly a colourful and eccentric officer, who was far from out of place in the BEF of 1914. In October he was promoted to the rank of major-general, which always brought with it command of a division. Hunter Weston's first reaction when he learned of his promotion was instead to express the hope that he would stay in command of his brigade. His reputation as a general, despite his personal bravery, would never fully recover from the débâcle at Gallipoli, where his command of British and ANZAC forces was widely considered by many to be completely ineffectual. This damage to his reputation was compounded by the way he handled his corps during the Somme offensive in July 1916. On the first day of the battle his corps suffered grotesque casualties, partly due to the inadequate and hopelessly unrealistic nature of his operational plans. Nikolas Gardner, however, has rightly pointed out some of Hunter Weston's other redeeming qualities, including a well-defined sense of duty, honour and fair play, all of which would eventually be employed to Elkington's benefit later on.[183] During the later stages of the war he became a Conservative Member of Parliament for a Scottish constituency.

The identity of the other officers involved in the court martial remains unknown as whatever records existed were destroyed during the Blitz in 1940. The broad outline of the trial can nevertheless be pieced together by drawing on Elkington's and Mainwaring's own personal accounts and the 1914 *Manual of Military Law*. For any court martial Field Service Regulations required at least two members of similar or higher rank to the accused, while for the trial of a battalion commander it was laid down that as many members of the court as possible should have held an equivalent command. For Mainwaring and Elkington, it is very likely that at least one would have been a colonel from another brigade in the division, as only one colonel from 10 Brigade would have been available to sit as a member. Colonel Churcher, commanding the Royal Irish Fusiliers, had been relieved of his command by Haldane on 5 September, on the same day that Elkington had been arrested, and replaced by a major acting in a temporary capacity. Sir Evelyn Bradford, commanding the Seaforth Highlanders and a great favourite of Haldane's, was still in command of his battalion and could well have been a member of the court. He was tragically killed leading his battalion into action two days later.

Elkington claimed that he was 'taken straight to my trial after a long day's march'. The war diary of the Royal Warwickshires for 12 September records a gruelling march that began at 5.30am from a farm a mile west of Villers-le-Petit and ended at Ecury. Over the previous few days the battalion had marched well over 30 miles. The weather was dreadful. On the day of the trial it rained hard all day long. It is not possible to be clear about when Mainwaring and Elkington were told the date of the court martial, or how much time they were given to prepare for it. At the very most they had a week in which to formulate a defence and assemble any witnesses, but neither man seems to have given any thought to doing either of these things.

According to the 1914 *Manual of Military Law*, the proceedings would have opened with Hunter Weston and the other court members swearing the following oath:

> I do swear that I will well and truly try the accused persons before the court according to evidence and that I will duly administer justice according to the Army Act now in force, without partiality, favour or affection ... so help me God.

Mainwaring and Elkington would then have been informed by the President of the Court of the charges against them and asked how they intended to plead. Both pleaded not guilty to both charges. They were then offered the chance to object to any member of the court, but it seems no such objection was made before the case was opened by the prosecution. At the time military law also conferred the right on an accused person to be represented by another person – a fellow officer – at a court martial. This right could be waived, however, and it is reasonable to assume that this is what Mainwaring and Elkington decided to do. It is hard to imagine that the court martial did not address this obvious procedural point at the beginning of the trial, although in these early days of the war field general courts martial did not have the benefit of a legally trained officer to advise them about proper procedure. Elkington was clear that neither he nor Mainwaring were represented: 'I had no one to help me in the defence of myself and the other colonel and was not in a fit state to think clearly.'

The prosecution case was presented by the Deputy Judge Advocate-General, Major Gilbert Mellor, who was himself a qualified lawyer. He had only been gazetted two weeks earlier and came from the reserve of officers mobilised for war. It is not clear which prosecution witnesses gave evidence at the trial. In his autobiography Tom Bridges makes no reference to doing so, nor does Osburn or any of the other eye-witnesses to the events in St Quentin on 27 August. General Snow thought that witnesses had been called, and that they had been travelling with Elkington and Mainwaring before the trial commenced – which would in itself have been a rather unusual procedure – but gave no indication about their identity.[184] They may well have been soldiers from their respective battalions, who might have been able to confirm some of the basic facts, such as whether a surrender document had been signed, and what orders each colonel had given their men.

It is equally unclear how vigorously the cowardice charge was prosecuted and whether Major Mellor chose to rely more on the charge of scandalous conduct to secure the conviction he sought. To obtain a conviction for cowardice, Mellor would have to have shown that the alleged acts of cowardice were committed in the presence of the enemy, in accordance with Section 4 of the Army Act which specified an offence of 'misbehaving in front of the enemy in such a way as to show cowardice'. He would certainly have faced an uphill task in persuading the court to convict on this charge. 'Misbehaviour' in these circumstances meant that the accused person, from an unsoldierlike regard for his own safety, failed in respect of some distinct and feasible duty imposed on him by a specific order or regulation, or by the well understood custom of the army.[185]

Although the concept of cowardice was not overtly spelt out in the Army Act, two essential elements had to be present to sustain a conviction. First, the offence had to be committed in the presence of the enemy. Secondly, the act or actions had to be motivated by fear of the enemy. In the case of Mainwaring and Elkington, enemy troops were certainly in the vicinity of St Quentin although not in the town itself when the surrender was attempted. Both officers were clearly aware of the proximity of the Germans, Mainwaring particularly so. But it is hard to see what evidence there was in their behaviour at St Quentin that could possibly have supported the second essential ingredient to the charge of cowardice. Mellor was certainly not able to argue that Elkington's and Mainwaring's behaviour at St Quentin was primarily motivated by fear of the enemy, for the simple reason that it was not. They were certainly fearful of the damage that the enemy might inflict on the civilian population of the town but this was not the same thing as fearing for their own personal safety or for that of their men. But it was a significant charge to level against the two colonels and reflected GHQ's very serious disapproval of their actions on the 27th.

In due course both colonels were, rightly, acquitted of the charge of cowardice. The court members showed little appetite for challenging their behaviour on this ground, especially as they had before them another route whereby their disapproval could be more easily signalled. Even so, their acquittal on this charge was not a foregone conclusion. Preparations had been made for every possible outcome. On the morning of 12 September Ben Clouting, a private with Tom Bridges' 4th Royal Dragoon Guards, was put on alert for membership of a firing squad:

> The regiment was on the outskirts of a town when I was one of eleven troopers and a corporal called to fall in with our rifles by one of our sergeants. We were given no explanation and although we asked the sergeant we were none the wiser. Told to wait on a street corner until further orders. We hung around for a couple of hours before abruptly being stood down. Nothing was said. I was curious and waited for the first opportunity to ask the sergeant what it was all about. He told me that we were to shoot two lieutenant colonels had a court martial passed death sentences on them. Instead the court martial adjudged both to have had a mental breakdown owing to severe stress and cashiered them.[186]

The charge of scandalous conduct under Section 16 of the Army Act gave the court an altogether easier and more convenient option. The surrender document would almost certainly have been the critical piece of evidence as it was an attempt by Mainwaring, acting apparently under Elkington's orders, to surrender the men under their command to the Mayor of St Quentin without those troops being in direct contact with the enemy. It would have been a different story if Elkington and Mainwaring had been forced to surrender by superior enemy forces. But an attempt to surrender their men to a civic official, of all people, when the enemy was nowhere in sight and without specific sanction from their superior officers was something else altogether. The retreat from Mons had been a fighting retreat and this was very much how the army wanted to portray it. Many battalions had fought long and hard to protect their retreating comrades from the Germans, and some had been overwhelmed in the process. The events at St Quentin represented a very different interpretation – that of a disorganised shambles, with some British troops throwing in the towel, having lost the will to fight. This would have been a propaganda triumph for the Germans, and would inevitably have damaged morale at home as well as in the BEF. Elkington and Mainwaring stood accused of orchestrating an act that to army eyes was unforgivable.

The two colonels' defence was a clumsy one. In seeking to surrender to the mayor, their motivation had simply been to avoid unnecessary civilian casualties. Elkington claimed that he tried to accept sole responsibility for what happened: 'As senior officer, I took the full blame of any mistakes made and asked for Colonel Mainwaring's acquittal as I was sure he was not in a fit state to be tried.'

This brief account is all that remains as evidence about the nature of the defence case at the trial. It does not appear that they called any witnesses in their defence. Both colonels would have addressed the court in their own defence, in Elkington's case using the notes he had prepared as an *aide-mémoire*. The charge against them alleged that they had acted together, and so for both to have been convicted the court must have been persuaded that Elkington had indeed ordered Mainwaring to surrender.

The rules of procedure dictated by military law required that the court's verdict on the most junior officer be declared first, followed by the others in order of seniority. In the case of Elkington and Mainwaring the decision was unanimous. In all probability, the outcome in this case was a foregone conclusion even before the court had heard the evidence. The military authorities had already come to a conclusion about Elkington and Mainwaring, whose behaviour, in their view, was so serious that only a court martial could administer a suitably appropriate penalty. In this context, it is hard to imagine that the members of the court martial had any doubt what was expected of them, notwithstanding the oath they swore to try the accused 'without partiality, favour or affection'. Other options than summoning a court martial were open to the higher command. The example of Colonel Churcher, who was relieved of his command and sent back to England after disappointing Haldane by his behaviour during the retreat, was one such option. This route would have involved no publicity and very little fuss. Matters would have been brushed under the carpet and reputations left largely intact. Both colonels could have been given other duties at home and faded from sight. Had the higher command chosen to treat it in this way, the episode at St Quentin would hardly have merited a footnote in the history of the retreat from Mons. However, this option was clearly not thought to represent a sufficiently serious rebuke, given the magnitude of Elkington's and Mainwaring's misbehaviour. Churcher might have been an inadequate leader in the field, as were many other battalion commanders in 1914, but Elkington's and Mainwaring's mistakes were in an altogether different category – theirs was a serious lapse of judgement coupled with a complete failure of command. But their joint defence of avoiding unnecessary civilian deaths was rejected, and no allowance at all was made for their physical and mental state. It is interesting to speculate whether the outcome would have been any different if Osburn had been able to testify. It seems unlikely, as the army clearly required its pound of flesh.

The prosecution alleged that the two officers had no 'due cause' in deciding to surrender and the members of the court clearly agreed. Elkington's argument that he, as the senior officer, should be held fully responsible for Mainwaring's actions equally cut little ice. This argument would certainly have been undermined anyway if, as seems likely, he used the notes he had prepared for the trial, in which he made it clear he had not given Mainwaring any order to surrender. If he made this claim, then it is clear that the members of the court did not believe him, otherwise the charge of 'acting together' to surrender their men could not have stood up – one or other of them would have been guilty but not both. The sentence of the court was that they be cashiered. Their rank was stripped from them, as was their entitlement to wear medals. Both were now reluctant civilians.

Hunter Weston referred to the decision of the court martial in a letter he wrote in November to his wife: 'I was very sorry for them but that did not prevent me doing my duty and marking the enormity of their offence from a military point of view.'[187] In later correspondence with Elkington, Hunter Weston remarked that he felt both officers had suffered from a 'moment of mental aberration' in deciding to surrender their men to the mayor,[188] a view that closely corresponds to what Private Clouting was told by his sergeant. It is possible to infer from this that Hunter Weston may well have expressed some sympathy for the two defendants before informing them of the verdict of the court. Mainwaring alluded to this in his statement written after the trial, when he referred to the exhausted state of his men: 'The limit of their endurance had been reached. *Their condition was admitted by the Court, by mouth of the President.*'

For Major Mellor, conducting his first significant military trial of the war, this court martial must have been a powerful introduction to the reality of combat in these new conditions. These and other trials later on provided him with a unique insight into the combat-induced stress that many soldiers would endure on the Western Front. After the war Mellor was appointed to the Committee of Inquiry into Shell Shock under Lord Southborough, which in 1922 made recommendations on how this condition should be treated by the army. Interestingly, one of the committee's proposals was that expert advice should always be obtained when any medical question or doubt arose either before or during trials for serious military offences or in any subsequent review of the court's proceedings. Elkington's principal argument during the trial was that Mainwaring was not in a fit mental or physical state on 27 August and therefore could not be held accountable for his actions at St Quentin. It is fairly clear, however, that no attempt was made to examine this argument in any detail.

There is one strange dimension to the events at St Quentin on 27 August, which is that Elkington's and Mainwaring's behaviour attracted little criticism, and in fact provoked strong sympathy, among those who witnessed those events. Elkington and Mainwaring had some surprising allies, Tom Bridges among them. He felt the whole incident at St Quentin was down to the exhaustion of the men and nothing else: 'I quote this unpleasant incident to show to what extremes good troops will be driven by fatigue.'[189] Arthur Osburn took a similar view: 'What could the remnants of broken infantry do before the advance of a victorious army, whose cavalry could have mopped them up in an hour.' In fact, Osburn considered that to surrender was the brave thing to do in the circumstances. The commanders were two middle-aged and exhausted men, and judging from their appearance they were suffering from the severe effects of prolonged exposure to the sun.

Mainwaring himself, entirely convinced he had done the right thing throughout, ended his own recollections of the events at St Quentin with an interesting epilogue:

> What the men think of the matter may be judged from the following extract from a letter from an officer in my late regiment, who, unsolicited by me, is collecting evidence in the hope that it may be used when peace is declared. 'There is not a man here that does not believe implicitly in you and what you did to save them. There are several men in the other regiments now who swear that you alone saved them, so I am collecting as much information as possible which will assist in bringing things to light when this show is over.'

Unfortunately for Mainwaring, nothing came of this subsequent attempt to clear his name.

Perhaps the two colonels' biggest supporter was General Snow himself, who was told of the events at St Quentin on the day he received the order to place them under arrest. Some of the 'facts' he was given were slightly distorted. But he made a number of important observations, including the detail that the men were 'hungry and thoroughly done up. The men could go no further ... they were dead to the world.'[190] Snow was also told that the surrender document had been drawn up between the two colonels on the one part and the German Emperor on the other: 'Now it is very difficult to know what else Colonel Mainwaring could have done. He could not get his men to their legs to move out of the town, his was much too small a party to hold the town, therefore he had to give himself and his men up as prisoners.'

Snow knew Mainwaring reasonably well. He described him as a man of a 'rather theatrical nature' and one can see him saying 'at any rate they will always quote my actions as the proper thing to do in such circumstances'. Overall Snow concluded that,

> as far as I can see, Mainwaring behaved perfectly properly. All through the war the correct thing to do depended on the point of view of one's immediate senior. Often men found themselves in an isolated position and retired. It was just even betting

whether they got DCMs for gallant conduct in a difficult position or whether they were shot for cowardice.[191]

Snow clearly felt that the two colonels should not have been prosecuted at all. But he was in no position either to influence the outcome of the court martial or to decide whether a prosecution should have taken place in the first place. In this regard, the same is true of Osburn and Bridges, although it is interesting to speculate what the outcome might have been if all three had been called as witnesses. Might it have been possible for them to insist that Elkington and Mainwaring were not responsible for their actions at St Quentin? And if so, when was the precise moment when they became unfit to exercise command? Even while they were clearly at the limits of their physical endurance, the two officers were still making sound and reasonable decisions. They had led their men and maintained discipline during the difficult march to St Quentin. Mainwaring had tried to secure food and water for his men. Elkington had sought to arrange transport. They were, in short, both in control of their emotions. The principal issue for the court seems to have been the simple and uncontested fact that an attempt had been made to surrender to the enemy when the men under the command of the two colonels were not in contact with the enemy. Their motivation for doing so was not considered relevant by Hunter Weston and his fellow court members. No officer and gentleman would have considered doing any such thing.

As far as the trial process itself is concerned, the conduct of proceedings can be criticised on two substantive counts. First, neither of the accused was given a reasonable opportunity to prepare for the trial and mount a credible defence, especially in terms of introducing evidence concerning their physical and mental health. Secondly, there was no proper legal representation. Taken together, these points begin to make the trial look seriously deficient. It almost certainly would not have met current standards of due process. However, the British Army was fighting a war at the time of the court martial and the circumstances did not permit the application of higher civilian standards. Senior commanders engaged in the conduct of active operations could hardly have been taken away for long periods to preside over judicial proceedings. They were needed in the field with their troops.

It could be plausibly argued that Elkington and Mainwaring were the recipients of rough justice. The real question, however, is whether there was enough justice on display at Chouy on 12 September 1914 to avoid any suggestion that they were victims of a kangaroo court. Elkington and Mainwaring were at least able to rebut the more serious of the two charges brought against them. Is this sufficient to give the whole process the benefit of the doubt? Ultimately, the answer to this question rests on how seriously the cowardice charge was put forward by the prosecution. In the absence of any surviving records, this is impossible to determine. The cowardice charge levelled against the colonels might very easily have been dropped early on in the trial by Mellor in favour of the second charge, on which he must have been much more confident about securing a conviction. The verdict was predictable enough, but a gross miscarriage of justice was certainly avoided by the defendants' acquittal on the cowardice charge.

The court martial's condemnation of the attempted surrender was clear and unambiguous, and in the process the army obtained the result it wanted. A clear line had been drawn in the sand. The behaviour of the two senior officers was judged to have been unacceptable in the circumstances. The commander-in-chief promptly confirmed the sentence. As far as the army was concerned, the case was closed. But Elkington chose not to follow Mainwaring's example and accept a decline into gentle obscurity, and his refusal to do so meant that historical interest in the treatment of both colonels would persist and they would remain a subject of continued controversy.

Chapter 6

Elkington's Redemption, Mainwaring's Resignation

Whate'er was dear before is dearer now.
There's not a bird singing upon his bough
But sings the sweeter in our English ears:
There's not a nobleness of heart, hand, brain
But shines the purer; happy is England now
In those that fight, and watch with pride and tears.

John Freeman, 'Happy is England Now'

After the trial Elkington and Mainwaring were placed in custody for two days, under constant shell fire, according to Elkington, from German guns on the heights above the River Aisne, before being sent home in disgrace. The circumstances of their return journey to England were not recorded. They would almost certainly have been escorted under armed guard on to one of the cross-Channel ferries and then left to make their own way home as soon as they landed in England. It is not clear whether either of them were met by friends or family. It is more likely they travelled up to London on their own. Given the vagaries of war-time transport arrangements, it would have been very difficult to coordinate their arrival in the UK. They would almost certainly have travelled in civilian clothing since they were no longer officers.

Elkington and Mainwaring arrived in England under an enormous cloud that would get darker by the minute. The last ten days had been difficult enough, and both men must have been at the lowest point of their professional and personal lives. Under close arrest by soldiers of their own regiments, they had followed their battalions as they made their highly significant advance up to the Marne but without being able to take any part in the fighting as the BEF pushed the Germans back nearly

40 miles. From being active participants, they had become powerless bystanders in the most important military operation of their time in the army. The agony of the court martial and the abrupt ending of their military careers would soon be followed by further humiliation as their fate was about to become public knowledge. The decision of the court martial was promulgated to the army in Routine Order 88 of 14 September 1914. The sentence of the court was also confirmed in the *London Gazette* on 30 October and this was followed by several articles in the national press the following day. There was no hiding place, no safe haven for either of them. At a time when the whole country was gearing up for the biggest military campaign it had ever fought, these two career soldiers, both in the prime of their professional lives, found themselves redundant and on the side lines. They had come back to England in disgrace, stripped of the command of their battalions and shorn of all rank and medals. Nearly thirty years of service to their king and country had ended in shame and dishonour.

Elkington came straight home to his country seat at Purley Hall outside Pangbourne in Berkshire. Here, in the safe and comfortable surroundings of his family home, he could decide what to do next. His wife Mary had just given birth to their second child, a daughter called Jean, and he would at least have the consolation of being able to spend some time with her – something that would have been impossible if he were still on active service. For Elkington, however, this was little compensation for what he had lost.

Elkington faced a clear choice that autumn. He could have resigned himself to his fate and settled into the quiet life of a country gentleman. His private income was sufficient, so there were no immediate financial concerns for him or his family to worry about. Life would, after all, go on. He had a large dairy farm that needed attending to. He could, quite easily, take up an active part in his local community and in supporting various charitable causes. He could even have chosen to spend more time with his family, although this would have been an unusual option for a man like him. He could also have expected any public ignominy and disgrace associated with his court martial to die down eventually. The newspapers had plenty of other war stories to write about. The public might have been prepared to forget about the whole matter and possibly even forgive him once they heard his side of the story. This would, of course, take time and effort and there was no certainty of a positive outcome. In any event, mounting such a public defence had the obvious downside of drawing even further attention to his case. The court of public opinion is a fickle thing at best and at the beginning of such a national emergency, whose side would people most probably take? For Elkington, it soon became clear that a forgive and forget strategy would not be enough. In fact, it was the last thing on his mind. A soldier's life was all that he knew, and wanted. The army had been his entire life. It mattered to him above and beyond everything else. He was a soldier first, a father and country squire second.

So Elkington made an early decision to reject the quiet life and the easy option of sinking into comfortable obscurity with his family in rural Berkshire and opted instead to attempt to restore his reputation as a soldier. In coming to this decision he had the full support and backing of his wife and family. The difficult question was how to go about it. He could not rejoin the British Army as an officer, as a commission was simply not open to him. Nor could he re-enlist as a private soldier as he was too old. Had conscription been in operation in the autumn of 1914, he might have found his way back into the army through this route. But conscription was still some way off and Elkington was not to know then whether it would ever be a serious possibility. But time was of the essence. He needed to act quickly if he were to save his reputation.

For a man desperate to prove himself again as a soldier, there really was only one choice open to him, and that was to enlist in the army of one of Britain's allies. Russia was too far away and an altogether too complicated option. There was no tradition of foreigners enlisting in the Tsar's army. The obvious choice for Elkington was the French Army. It appears that such a course of action was on his mind from the beginning. The author of an article about Elkington that appeared in a British newspaper in September 1916 quoted a friend of the colonel's as saying that as soon as he returned to England after the court martial he had told him 'there is still the Foreign Legion'.

Foreigners who wanted to serve in the French Army had, since 1831, been able to join the Foreign Legion, although at that time they were not allowed to serve in any other regiments or units of the French Army or Navy. The Legion had been established as a mercenary unit designed to fight France's colonial wars, and although it had a duty to try to integrate the legionnaires into French society, few chose to take this route. As a result, the Legion had developed a sinister reputation as a haven for Europe's social outcasts. It was also a safe harbour for criminals evading justice, who could bask in anonymity in a secretive organisation that fiercely protected its own from any outside intrusion. To the French military authorities, the Legion had become something of a ghetto – a holding pen for some of Europe's most unruly and dangerous individuals, and they therefore did their best to keep it at arm's length from the main body of the French Army. It served in Indo-China, Algeria and Morocco, in fact anywhere but France itself. When the First World War broke out, the Legion had four battalions in Algeria, three in Tonkin and five in Morocco, and numbered just over 10,000 officers and men. The Legion would soon double in size, however, as its numbers were swelled by a wave of eager new recruits, who came from rather more respectable backgrounds than those the Legion traditionally welcomed.

In August 1914 Paris was a great metropolitan city, with a wide and diverse population of resident foreign nationals. As soon as war was declared, many of them were quick to express their eagerness to serve in the French cause. The French Government decided on 3 August to take advantage of this surge in foreign support by allowing non-French nationals to enlist for the duration of the war. The one caveat was that there would be no change to the rule that required foreign nationals to serve in the Foreign Legion.

These new recruits enlisted out of their love for France and their support for the wider Allied cause. Some were attracted by the apparent glamour and excitement of the heroic and romantic defence of democracy and the notion of safeguarding the freedoms of the smaller nations of Europe against the tyranny of Prussian militarism. These idealistic new volunteers were therefore of a very different type and quality to the ones traditionally accepted into the Legion. On the whole they were men of good character, often quite affluent, many of them from the professional classes or the skilled working class. Many were intellectuals. Others were highly political émigrés from other European states where they had been persecuted because of their ethnic or political views. In many ways Elkington would have been a very good example of this new type of legionnaire. And like many of these new recruits, he would find himself in a completely alien environment that was unlike anything he had experienced during his own extensive military career.

A general mobilisation was declared in Paris on 1 August. In a city already bursting with patriotism and national fervour, on that day a group of foreign nationals led by the Swiss writer Blaise Cendrars announced that: 'The hour is grave. Every man worthy of his name must act today, must forbid himself to remain inactive in the midst of the most formidable conflagration that history has ever experienced.' On 5 August a similar declaration made to Americans in Paris by the Chicago-born Rene Phelizot in support of the French cause brought forward numerous volunteers, including two Harvard graduates, Henry Farnsworth and Alan Seeger, the famous war poet and author of *I Have a Rendezvous with Death*. At the beginning of the war both men were trying to pursue careers as writers. Seeger was already in Paris but Farnsworth was working in Mexico City and immediately packed his bags and left for France as soon as war was declared.

These declarations had an electrifying effect in Paris itself, where the atmosphere was already supercharged. Russian émigrés began drilling in a cinema they had hired on the Rue de Tolbiac. A large group of Jewish people paraded in the Place de la Bastille to demonstrate their support for France and signal their willingness to fight her enemies under the banner of the Tricolour. Romanians opened a recruiting office in a café on the rue Mercadet. British residents in Paris were invited to the Imperial Club for a meeting, the purpose of which was the formation of a British volunteer corps that would offer its services to the French Government. Potential American recruits to the Legion went through their military paces in the gardens of the Palais Royal, while British volunteers made use of the 'Magic City' amusement park. By the end of August formal recruitment began. Volunteers began reporting in national groups to the Hotel des Invalides, where they underwent a physical examination before signing their enlistment papers. Once the formalities were done with, the groups were marched away under their own national colours to the various railway stations in the city to join their units and begin their formal training. On 25 August the American contingent, about 50 strong, followed the American flag – carried alternately by Seeger and Phelizot – through a cheering crowd of Parisians up the Avenue de L'Opera and the rue Auber to the Gare Saint-Lazarre on their way to their new barracks at Toulouse.

This outpouring of foreign support for France must have been a powerful boost to national morale at a vital time in the war. The results of the early battles were not encouraging for the Allied cause. A general retreat was under way to the north and Paris itself was in danger of falling to the Germans. The French Government had already left the city for Bordeaux. The 'Battle of the Frontiers' in Alsace and Lorraine had ended in enormous losses and yet with no territorial advantage to the French of any kind. Nevertheless, this rush to join the Legion represented a victory of sorts in the propaganda campaign. Indeed, so popular was the Allied cause that thousands of men from around the world were signing up to defend France and her Allies. In contrast, Germany and the Central Powers could claim no such success.

Exactly how many foreigners enlisted with the Legion is not, however, entirely clear. Legion statistics show that a total of 42,883 foreign nationals enlisted during the course of the war, with numbers rising from 10,521 men in 1913 to 17,147 by the end of 1914, eventually peaking at just under 22,000 in 1915. Numbers fell away significantly in subsequent years, particularly when the Italians joined the war in the spring of 1915. In fact, about 5,000 of the initial recruits were Italian – enough to form a separate *regiment de marche* under an Italian commander. A similar number of Russians joined up. A battalion of nearly a thousand men from Greece enlisted in early 1915 and were known as the *bataillon de marche etranger d'Orient*. A similar number were recruited from amongst émigré Montenegrins. Fifty-three Japanese citizens also came forward to serve.

The Legion had to make drastic changes in order to cope with this sudden rush of new recruits. The Algerian battalions were ordered to send half of their numbers to France to begin the work of assimilating the new legionnaires. They would help establish three new Legion regiments, the 2e, 3e and 4e *regiments de marche* of the 1er *etranger*. The 3e regiment was recruited mainly from foreigners resident in Paris, and was the unit that Elkington eventually joined in 1915. Until the Legion was able to furnish the new regiment with its own leaders, these were initially provided by army reservists employed in the Paris fire brigade. There was, in fact, no other obvious alternative source of supply as Regular and Territorial army officers and NCOs tended to give the Legion a very wide berth because of its seedy reputation and overt hostility to anyone who was not from the Legion.

Henry Farnsworth and Alan Seeger joined the 3e regiment in the autumn of 1914. According to Farnsworth, it was composed of men who belonged to 'the most sedentary professions'. As for the Legion as a whole, Farnsworth was not overly impressed: 'It is not much like its reputation. Many of the men are educated and the very lowest is of the high-class workman type.' The NCO in command of his own squad was a 'militant socialist' who violently berated those from more affluent backgrounds. As for the Parisian firemen, they were good drill masters but as campaign leaders they were 'nothing but a nuisance'. Victor Chapman, another American serving alongside Seeger in the *3e etranger*, had a similar opinion of his superiors, claiming that 'we were disreputably officered in the *3e de marche*'.

The arrival of the experienced Legionnaires from Algeria would come as a profound shock to many of the new recruits. Hardened veterans of numerous bloody colonial campaigns, they were steeped in the traditions of the old Legion and had little sentiment or sympathy for the new men and their concept of the noble cause. Alan Seeger recalled the difficult transition that began to take place as the eager new Legionnaires began their training:

> the majority of the men who engaged voluntarily were thrown
> in a regiment made up almost entirely of the dregs of society,
> refugees from justice and roughs, commanded by *sous-officers*
> who treated us all without distinction in the same manner that
> they were habituated to treat their unruly brood in Africa.

The harshness of life in the Legion for these new recruits soon became common knowledge. As early as November 1914 the French Military Attaché in London received a letter from a former member of parliament for Dartford, protesting bitterly about the treatment of his nephew, who had lived in Paris for many years and had enlisted as soon as war was declared:

The composition and character of this regiment is only too well known. I feel sure that it could not be the desire of the French Government to place young men of good character amongst the scum of Europe. My nephew writes that he is willing to fight to give his life if needs be amongst French or English regulars, but that existence is 'hell on earth' in the midst of bad characters by whom he and his comrades are surrounded. They don't ask to be relieved of their military duties, but to be treated as men and not outcasts.[192]

The new recruits endured violence, theft and abuse, often initiated by the NCOs. Conflict between the various national groupings also led to further outbreaks of bad discipline in the Legion: 'The New York papers do not exaggerate when they say this Legion is a fighting crowd,' wrote Russell Kelly, a graduate of the Virginia Military Institute in March 1915. 'There are just enough of each nationality so that one country fights another.'[193]

Lurking behind this poor treatment lay the different cultures that separated the old Legionnaires from those who had volunteered for the duration of the war. The old Legionnaires could not believe that the new recruits had joined in order to fight for a cause they believed in rather than for other, lesser, motives of the sort more commonly associated with enlistment in the Legion. The resulting tension remained a feature of life in the Legion for the entire period of the war and would play its part in the difficulties the Legion experienced in maintaining the highest levels of morale. Many of the foreign nationals who enlisted with such enthusiasm in the summer of 1914 were desperately trying to leave by the spring of 1915, either to join their own national armies or to move into French army regiments of the line. In the late summer of 1915, for example, Alan Seeger wrote:

I feel more and more the need of being among Frenchmen, where the patriotic and military tradition is strong, where my good will may have some recognition and where the demands of a sentimental and romantic nature like my own may be gratified.

Eventually the French Government would allow foreign nationals to serve in regular line regiments, thus correcting the initial lack of imagination in the way their enthusiasm to fight for France was handled. The ancient law requiring all foreigners to join the Legion represented a fundamental mistrust of their intentions and motives, which in the conditions of August 1914 seemed hopelessly out of place. However, despite all these difficulties, the performance of the Foreign Legion on the Western Front during the First World War was among the very best in the French Army. The fighting powers of the *regiment de marche de la legion etranger* made it one of only two regiments to earn both the Legion of Honour and the Croix de Guerre. Only four other regiments would be awarded the Medal Militaire. Only one other regiment was cited more times in army orders. In the desperate fighting at Carency, Navarin Farm, Hill 140 and Verdun the Legion earned the highest praise for valour and courage. This was the complicated, unusual but exceptionally heroic organisation that Elkington would soon become part of.

Having made the decision to join the French Army, Elkington spent the next few months at Purley Hall with his family. His movements during this period are not known, and nor is it clear when he came to his decision. All of the published accounts claim that Elkington returned to France almost immediately[194] but this is not true. Elkington enlisted in the Legion in Paris on 15 February 1915, almost five months to the day since his court martial.[195] He gave as his place of residence not Purley Hall but 5 Rue des Capucines, a prosperous boulevard close to Place de L'Opera in Paris. It is not clear whether he actually resided at this address, and if so, for how long. As it was not necessary to be resident in France in order to join the Legion, it can be assumed that he did live in Paris for a time. There is a suggestion that he was trying to lay a false trail about his real identity, but if this were the case, he would surely not have used his real name when he enlisted. In an interview Elkington gave to *The Times* in September 1916, he was asked about his enlistment and whether he had used his own name: 'Why of course. It would not have done for me to have taken another man's name.'

When he joined the Legion, Elkington made no reference to his career in the British Army or the rank he had held. His age and date of birth were accurately recorded. At 48, he was not considered too old to serve.

He enlisted as a private soldier, second class, and the next day joined his company, B3, as soldier number 29274. He was immediately posted to the 1st Battalion of the 3e regiment, where he met up with another new recruit, the American surgeon David Wheeler, who would become his closest friend in the Legion. Originally from Buffalo, New York, Wheeler was a graduate of Columbia University. He had arrived in France towards the end of 1914 and had served with his wife, also a doctor, in the French Red Cross. It was action he craved, however, and he enlisted in the Legion in Paris just a few days before Elkington. They were sent away together for their initial training in the Rhone valley. Elkington later described his first encounter with Wheeler:

> There was an American with me, called Wheeler, a famous surgeon. I met him first time marching up to the front. I thought he was a tramp and I expect he thought I was one. When we got to Lyons I went down to have a meal in the big hotel. There I saw the American sitting over a big dinner and he saw me. From that time on we were friends. We saw that neither was a tramp. We marched together, ate together and became great pals.[196]

Many of the new recruits to the Legion, Elkington included, would complete their initial training and introduction to trench warfare at Valbonne, a village near Lyons. Even taking into account the need for improvisation at this stage of the conflict, the conditions at Valbonne were rudimentary in the extreme. The camp was little more than row upon row of vermin-infected huts situated in a quagmire of mud. For someone like Elkington, these conditions must have severely tested his commitment to his new corps. Many of the American recruits in particular found the training not just extreme but totally inadequate. Most of the time was spent either on long route marches or on the rifle range. Few skills were learned that would help them survive the rigours of the trenches. The equipment with which they were issued was primitive and belonged to a different era. The standard rifle of the French Army in 1914 was the 1886-vintage 8mm Lebel. In the conditions of trench warfare, the Lebel very quickly jammed and became unusable and was therefore enormously unpopular with those who had to rely upon it to defend themselves from the enemy. It also suffered from a major design defect. Its eight rounds were loaded, nose to tail fashion, in a tubular magazine placed under the barrel of the rifle, and the magazine was not clip-loaded. This meant that the rifle was very slow to load, unlike the standard British rifle, the short magazine Lee Enfield. In addition, the operator had to be very wary of one round hitting the primer of the cartridge in front, causing a very unwelcome explosion in the chamber. Training was further hampered by the inevitable language differences between the instructors and the new recruits, few of whom spoke good French.

The 3e regiment had originally been sent to the Somme front near Santerre in December 1914. This was a quiet part of the line that saw very little heavy fighting, although casualties were incurred in the endless patrolling and raiding. During the winter and spring a 'live and let live' mentality had developed in the trenches. Both sides were exhausted by the heavy fighting of the last few months and the harsh winter gave each army the opportunity to build up its strength for the fighting that would inevitably start up again later in the spring, when the weather conditions would be more favourable for offensive operations. The regiment was by now over 2,000 strong, and was made up largely of Russian, Italian and Belgian volunteers. According to Elkington, there were very few Englishmen in the regiment. In the five months that had elapsed since his court martial, the nature of the war had changed beyond all recognition. The war of manoeuvre and rapid advances had been transformed into the static stalemate of trench warfare. During the course of the winter the trenches had inevitably become waterlogged, little more than channels for an ocean of mud. The first experience of the trenches for many of these new Legionnaires would have been very similar to that of Blaise Cendrars:

> We waded in mud up to the ankles, even to the knees, and glutinous clods, which detached themselves from the lips of the trench when we brushed by them, slid disagreeably down our necks. And as in a nightmare, we were impeded at every step ... The men were falling about, slithering, swearing, colliding with one another amidst a great clatter of hardware and mess tins. It was a case of two steps forward and one back.

The living conditions were miserable: 'collapsing dug-outs, crumbling parapets, disembowelled and scattered sandbags, tangled links of barbed wire and the shallow beginnings of slimy, nauseating trenches. There was a terrible stink of shit ...'.[197]

Life in the trenches hardly lived up to the glamorous image of battle the new recruits would have brought with them into the Legion. The same was probably true for every soldier who served in the war, on both sides. Trench warfare soon established its own grim and deadly routine. The soldiers manning the front-line trenches mounted early morning and evening alerts in readiness for any enemy attack. These periods of heightened tension were then followed by long hours spent trying to catch up on as much sleep as possible under whatever cover could be found. In the dank recesses dug into the walls of the trenches, the men shared more than each other's company, as lice and other vermin began to make their presence felt. During the hours of darkness no-man's-land had to be patrolled, supplies brought up and repairs made to the earthworks that gave the men their only, albeit limited, protection from the shelling and machine-gun fire of an often invisible enemy, who had himself disappeared into the bowels of the earth on his side of the line. This was a very different world from August 1914 and the opening salvoes of the war.

The first encounters between the new Legionnaires and the enemy left a powerful impression on these idealistic warriors. The Germans had clear weapon superiority and an abundance of ammunition of all sorts. The enemy were also, by common consent, better equipped for trench warfare. Cendrars felt that the 'German patrols had a lot of bite, being better equipped than ours', and Alan Seeger agreed that in trench warfare 'the Germans are marvellous'.

The 3e regiment did not in fact exist for very long. In the summer of 1915 foreign nationals were permitted to leave the Legion to join their own national armies, and so many went that in July it was decided to amalgamate the regiment with the *2e regiment de marche*. According to the records of the Legion, it seems that Elkington himself was transferred to the 2e regiment of the *1er regiment d'etranger* on 14 July as the new fighting season on the Western Front gathered a relentless momentum.

During the late winter of 1914 the German Army had begun to shift its focus away from the Western Front and on to the Eastern Front, where it hoped to land a decisive blow that would knock Russia out of the war. Several divisions were therefore moved east for the coming offensive. Britain and France both saw this as an opportunity to move on to the offensive. The French Commander-in-Chief, Joseph Joffre, planned to launch a number of assaults that were intended to split open the German defences and usher in the return of open warfare. Joffre's plan focused on eliminating the huge German 'bulge' into the French lines between Rheims and Amiens, as well as interrupting the vital transport lines and industrial infrastructure that lay just behind the German front lines. An important objective in this plan would be the recapture of the strategically important Vimy Ridge, which would give the French vital observation over the Domain plain, a heavily industrialised region that was vital to the German war effort. The French Army had, however, suffered grievous losses in the initial stages of the fighting and was still short of essential weapons and munitions. The quick-firing 75 guns were ideal for direct fire operations but less useful when it came to knocking out enemy gun positions hidden behind hills. They also had only a limited range, which made them less able to hit the reserve trenches. These, therefore, had to be attacked without the protection of covering artillery fire.

In pursuit of Joffre's wider plans, the Legion was ordered to attack Hill 140 on the northern shoulder of Vimy Ridge. On 9 May 1915, after a preliminary bombardment lasting 4 hours, three regiments of the *1er etranger*, with Elkington in their ranks, launched their attack. The first German line was quickly reached but moving further up the hill proved almost impossible. The advancing Legionnaires were exposed to murderous fire from machine-guns, artillery and mortars. Three of the battalion commanders were killed, as well as most of the company commanders. Notwithstanding these savage losses, the Legionnaires pressed on, largely leaderless and in small mixed-up units, to the top of the hill. They desperately needed reinforcements but these could not get through. The German infantry counter-attacked later in the afternoon, supported by accurate and sustained artillery fire, and eventually drove the Legionnaires back from the crest.

The day ended with the Legion still grimly holding on to the former German front line, but in all other respects the attack had failed to realise any of its objectives. The inexperience of these young, idealistic Legionnaires was one of the factors contributing to the extraordinarily high casualty figures. Almost 50 per cent of the regiment had been killed or wounded, with the losses amounting to nearly 2,000 men. The losses might perhaps have been lower had the attack not been conducted almost as a private affair, with very little liaison with any of the units on the Legion's flanks. In addition, during the advance, they had failed to ensure that all the defenders were properly accounted for. As a result they were just as likely to be fired on from the rear as from the front.

The fighting in this area would continue sporadically for several weeks. The legion launched another major attack on Vimy Ridge in June, this time suffering fewer casualties but with similarly disappointing results: the commanding heights of the ridge remained firmly in German hands. Elkington was in the thick of things throughout, in what was his first real fight of the war. On the crest of Hill 140, when their position came under heavy fire, Elkington led a group of men to help some of his comrades who were being mistakenly targeted by their own guns to the rear. A week later, when fighting erupted at Souchez, he eliminated a hidden machine-gun position before it could fire on some advancing Legionnaires.[198]

The enormous scale of the losses in the regiment provoked a crisis of morale in the 2e regiment. On 16 June some of the battalions refused to attack when ordered to do so, notably C Battalion, which was made up largely of Greek recruits who really wanted to fight the Turks, not the Germans. Most of the Italians were also released from service to join their own national army, and as a result by August the 2e regiment was gradually reduced from four battalions to two.

The fighting continued on the Western Front for most of the summer and into the autumn. On 28 September 1915 Elkington's regiment was given the task of assaulting the formidable German positions at Navarin Farm and Horseshoe Wood in the Champagne region near Rheims. American Legionnaire Edward Morlae provided a vivid, almost romantic, picture of the beginning of this epic battle:

> Then we left the cover of the trench, formed in Indian file, 50 metres between sections, and at the signal moved forward swiftly and in order. It was a pretty bit of tactics and executed with such a dispatch and neatness hardly equalled on the drill

ground. The first files of the sections were abreast, while the
men fell in, one close behind the other, and so we crossed the
ridge, offering the smallest possible target to the enemy's
guns.[199]

Shortly before the attack, Capitaine Junod, a veteran of many years'
service in the Legion, mounted the parapet in full dress uniform and
called out: 'Mes enfants, we are going to certain death, but we are going
to try to die like brave men.'

Edward Genet, an American descendant of a French revolutionary
leader, described what happened next:

We had started out to advance in solid columns of four, each
section in a unit. It was wonderful, that slow advance. Not a
waver, not a break. Through the storm of shell, the Legion
marched forward. One lost his personal feelings, he simply
became a unit, a machine.

Elkington and Wheeler, moving shoulder to shoulder, managed to get past
two lines of German barbed wire and into Horseshoe Wood. The trees
were splintering under artillery fire and bullets. The men edged forward,
using their grenades to clear out enemy positions. As he approached
Navarin Farm itself, a strongly fortified part of the enemy line, Elkington
was seriously wounded in the right leg by a burst of machine-gun fire.
Wheeler, who was alongside him at the time, was also wounded. They
collapsed together into a nearby shell-hole. In a later interview with *The
Times*, which was also reported in the *New York Times*, Elkington
recounted: '[Wheeler] gave me first aid and looking at my leg said, "I say,
old chap, they will have to take that off." Then he fainted across my leg
and hurt me like the devil.'

The bullets had shattered Elkington's shinbone and knee. It was a
potentially fatal injury and he was in agony. Wheeler gave him a shot of
morphine and helped stem the flow of blood, but Elkington would now
face over nine months of hospital treatment before he recovered sufficient
strength to travel back to England. He would never be fit for active service
again, but he was at least alive. This time the war really was over for
Elkington. Wheeler's wounds were not quite as severe, although his

service in the Legion would also now come to an end. At the time Elkington thought Wheeler's career as a soldier was over altogether, but Wheeler was not yet finished with the war. On his discharge from the Legion, he joined the Canadian Army and obtained the rank of captain. When the United States entered the war, he transferred to the US infantry. He died in action in July 1918.

Elkington was stretchered off the battlefield later that day, having spent over 12 hours in his shell-hole, and was sent to the Grenoble Military Hospital, where he was admitted on 1 October. The surgeons there, under the leadership of Dr Termier, carried out several major operations to save his leg. They succeeded, although the leg was left permanently damaged. On his arrival, Elkington's personal possessions were listed as one Kepi helmet, one pair of pantaloons and one shirt.

In recognition of his valour, Elkington was awarded the *Medal Militaire* on 16 June 1916, while recovering at Grenoble. The citation read:

> In spite of being 50 years old, he showed during the campaign a remarkable bravery and energy, giving the best example to others. He was seriously injured on 28 September, lunging forward to assault the enemy's trenches …

Elkington was also awarded the *Croix de Guerre avec palmes*. Paul Rockwell, another American who joined the Legion in August 1914, and who also served initially with Elkington in the 3e regiment, would later recall Elkington's account of the fighting during the Champagne offensive:

> During the first night of the Champagne attack, Wheeler showed his coolness. There was a false cry for us to charge and the third company, in which we were, started forward with fixed bayonets. The commandant of the battalion, seeing the mistake, jumped in front of the advancing and excited men and tried to check them. One of the sergeants helped him and Wheeler, with more sang-froid than the rest, also helped him. The check succeeded and the commandant took Wheeler's name. The commandant met a soldier's death directly in front of Wheeler during our attack on the 28th.

Perhaps unsurprisingly, given the secrecy of the Legion itself, Elkington's service with the Legion has given birth to many myths. Foremost among them is the suggestion that because of his bravery under fire he was rapidly promoted through the ranks and ultimately gained a commission. Tom Bridges, for example, thought that Elkington had become an officer,[200] while in John Parker's recent book *Inside the Foreign Legion* it is claimed that Elkington was 'promoted in the field to sergeant'.[201] There is no doubting Elkington's personal bravery or his courage under fire, but the records clearly show that Elkington remained a private soldier for the whole of his time in the Legion, content to serve alongside his fellows in the ranks.

On 26 August 1916 he was finally discharged from hospital and began his journey back to England, arriving at Purley Hall on Sunday, 3 September. After his return, the news soon spread that a former British lieutenant-colonel had fought in the French Foreign Legion as a private soldier and that he had been seriously wounded in an attack on the German trenches. Elkington gave interviews to the national press, including *The Times* and the *Daily Sketch*. In an interview published in *The Times*, Elkington commented on what he saw as the 'fuss' being made of his story: 'What else could a man do? I was cashiered and about a fortnight after the notice appeared in the papers I was in the ranks of the Foreign Legion.' Elkington's sense of timing had clearly deserted him, but his determination to claw back his reputation as a soldier was all too apparent from these remarks.

He also went on to recount some of his thoughts about the seven months he spent on active service with the Legion:

> It was hard work. We were nearly always in the thick of it. Many of the men in the Legion wore medals – medals of all the wars of the last twenty years. I cannot wear mine even if I wanted to. I was cashiered, and had no right to any of them.
>
> I don't think the men in the Legion fear anything. I never saw such men and I think that in the attack at Champagne they were perfectly wonderful. I never saw such a cool lot in my life as when they went forward to face the German fire. It was a great fight, they were all out for blood and although they were almost cut up there, they got the German trenches.

Elkington recalled that his identity was only ever compromised once:

> We were marching in the Champagne country and had just
> stopped to drink at a stream when a military motor went by.
> Someone in the car called out 'Hello Elkington' and I was afraid
> that I would be given away.

But the moment soon passed as Elkington failed to acknowledge his
erstwhile acquaintance, and he never revealed the identity of the British
officer travelling in the car. Seconds later, he resumed his march down the
dusty road with his anonymity intact.

It is clear that Elkington had not told the Legion he was a former
colonel in the British Army when he joined up in February 1915, as
there is no reference to this at all in his service records until after he was
wounded and was being treated at Grenoble hospital. But it is doubtful
whether it would have made any difference. In any case it is unlikely that
he would have been asked very much about his background. The Legion
was keen to take all comers into its ranks and this had always been its
approach to recruitment, which was booming with the outbreak of war
and the outpouring of sentiment towards France and the Allied cause. I
suspect that Elkington's use of the word 'afraid' was probably a figure
of speech more than anything else. The Legion obviously knew he was
English and so it would hardly have been surprising if a member of the
British armed forces had recognised him en route to the Front. This
alone would not have threatened his position in the Legion, although it
might have generated unwelcome publicity back home if the story got
out that he had enlisted again in order to fight the Germans. At some
point this fact would become public knowledge. Perhaps Elkington was
not yet ready for it to happen.

A few weeks before Elkington was discharged from hospital in
Grenoble, the news of his service in the Legion reached General Hunter
Weston, who was heavily immersed in the Battle of the Somme. To his
very great credit, Hunter Weston decided that Elkington's efforts to
salvage his honour and reputation deserved a suitably generous response
from the army. There was no reason for him to intercede in this way, and
he was in any case more than preoccupied with current operations. He

could quite easily have let events take their course and sort themselves out. However, he clearly felt some responsibility towards Elkington and decided to help him recover his rank and status in the British Army. His first thought was to secure him a pardon. He therefore spoke to the Adjutant-General, Lieutenant-General C.F.N. Macready. At the end of August he personally wrote to Elkington to say that he believed a pardon would be forthcoming. This proved to be a false hope, however. Elkington and Mainwaring had been charged with scandalous conduct in that they had both 'acted together' in seeking to surrender the men under their command. Pardoning one of the two officers involved in the original offence but not the other presented a difficulty. Mainwaring had, after all, done nothing to justify a pardon and could not fairly benefit from Elkington's heroics. A solution was, however, at hand. A notice appeared in both the *London Gazette* and *The Times* early in September announcing that: 'The King has approved of the reinstatement of John Ford Elkington in the rank of Lieutenant Colonel, with his previous seniority, in consequence of his gallant conduct while serving in the ranks of the Foreign Legion of the French Army.'

The king's decision appears to have been taken on 22 August, while Elkington was still in hospital at Grenoble.[202] A few weeks later, while still nursing his very serious leg injuries, he was invited to a private audience with the king at Buckingham Palace. On 28 October it was announced that Lieutenant-Colonel Elkington had been awarded the Distinguished Service Order. His reputation had now been restored to him, in just recognition of his undoubted bravery and determination. Elkington had walked a long and difficult road, one that very few men would have chosen to take. His journey to redemption was complete.

The injury to his leg made it impossible for him to resume his military career, as active service was completely out of the question. He retired from the army in the spring of 1919 and settled down with his family at their new home at Adbury Halt near Newbury. Colonel Elkington and his wife Margaret had a second son, Richard, in 1918. For most of the next 26 years John Elkington lived an active life. He became a local magistrate on the bench at Kingsclere and was involved in the work of the local hospital, where he was Chairman of the Board. He took a keen interest in the activities of the Newbury Air Training Corps.

The Second World War left its mark on the Elkington family. Jean's husband, an officer in the Grenadier Guards, was killed at Arnhem, while Richard died from wounds received while fighting with the Rifle Brigade in North Africa. Colonel Elkington himself died on 27 June 1944. In 1946 a stained-glass window in the Church of the Ascension in Burghclere was dedicated to his memory. Field-Marshal Montgomery performed the official opening. The *Newbury Weekly News* reported him as saying:

> We Britishers had a curious habit of never being set when great events happened in the world and we always started our affairs by having great disasters, which generally resulted in pulling certain people down with them. It so happened that John Ford Elkington was pulled down by disasters through no fault of his own and a good many others were too. But alone of them all, he fought back and made good, proving himself to be a great and gallant soldier. It can be said of him that he did his duty. Not only did he fight back, but he made good more than he lost.[203]

* * *

Mainwaring, in contrast to Elkington, completely disappeared from public sight. It is not clear how he spent the last 16 years of his life, and it is not known if there was ever any contact between the two men after their court martial. There was a rumour that he too had attempted to re-enlist in the Middlesex Regiment, but it was just a rumour. He was in very poor health and it is hard to see how he could possibly have passed a medical examination. In fact, it is doubtful whether he was truly fit for active service when the war was declared. In any event, he was too old to join up. By 1927 he and his wife Clarice were living in Melbourne, Derbyshire. At some point in the 1920s he suffered a severe stroke that left him paralysed down one side and with very limited speech. By 1930 he and Clarice were living at Pounsey Mill in Blackboys, Sussex. Arthur died there quietly, in the presence of his wife, on 11 October 1930.

The attempt by his fellow officers to restore his reputation, referred to in his personal statement, sadly never materialised. Why this was so is not clear. His correspondent at the time might simply have been trying to cheer him up with the prospect that an effort would ultimately be made to clear his name. In truth, it was always a forlorn hope. There was no avenue open to him at that point to challenge the verdict of the court martial and he had done nothing since his conviction to merit any discretionary mercy. It seems he spent the last few years of his life doing the things he enjoyed most – fishing, cricket and playing cards with his friends. He probably died still convinced of his innocence, knowing that all he had tried to do was to save innocent women and children from an unnecessary death and his own men from a pointless sacrifice.

Of the two colonels, Mainwaring had certainly displayed more of the symptoms of fatigue and distress at St Quentin on 27 August than Elkington. He was therefore perhaps more entitled than Elkington to receive the benefit of any doubt about his culpability. These must have been some of the thoughts that occupied his mind when he thought back to those four tumultuous days in France. Although neither colonel was ever pardoned for the crime, Elkington had at least died with the knowledge that he had re-established his good name. The same comfort and peace of mind would never be extended to Mainwaring, whose poor and declining health meant he was simply not in a position to take the course of action Elkington had chosen. At least Mainwaring continued to enjoy a wide and varied social life, surrounded by numerous friends and in the company of his beloved wife. Nothing suggests that his last few years were spent agonising or complaining over his 'unfair' treatment, or that he suffered any hardship as a result of it.

There are two sides to any story, and the court martial of Elkington and Mainwaring is no exception to this rule. The charitable view of their actions, which is perhaps the one many would subscribe to today, is based on three salient facts. First, that both men were acting without any clear intelligence of the enemy and his whereabouts, and without any contact with higher military authority. They were completely in the dark. Given all they had seen over the previous few days, was it unreasonable for them to assume the worst? That they were on their own, without the means to properly defend themselves against a catastrophic German assault on St Quentin and the heavy loss of human life that would inevitably follow? Secondly, they were both at the limits of their physical and mental endurance. Their judgements and decisions would inevitably be less than perfect as a result. Should this loss of capacity not have been reflected in a lesser sanction than being cashiered in disgrace? And thirdly, they were both acting under the influence of a noble impulse – to save the lives of innocent French civilians. When the reality of the situation was pointed out to them, they very quickly changed their minds about whether or not to surrender their men. In this context, their decisions take on a dimension of rationality that some observers would later argue could not fairly be described as 'scandalous'. This was the lenient view taken by those who witnessed at first hand the principal events at St Quentin – Bridges and Osburn in particular. Snow also felt that some other punishment would have been preferable to a court martial.

However, there is one twist in taking the charitable view. If the two colonels had simply been sent back to England with Colonel Churcher and either been quietly discharged or, more probably, found a desk job in the War Office, then Elkington's subsequent and extraordinary act of redemption would never have taken place at all. If the court martial's outcome was unfair, it was nevertheless the spur for Elkington to embark upon his mission to recover the honour that had been taken away from him. He would take advantage of this 'opportunity' in spectacular fashion. The court martial gave him the chance to rewrite his personal history, leaving a rich historical trail behind him. A quiet return to England would never have done so.

The uncharitable view rests on a very different foundation. The officers and men under their command had a clear and over-riding duty to fight the enemy. The two colonels bore the principal responsibility to see that this duty was discharged. By attempting to surrender when they did, they failed in their duty as officers. A fear of civilian casualties could never provide sufficient justification for failing to offer resistance to the enemy. After all, the recent fighting at Mons and Le Cateau had taken place in the presence of large numbers of civilians. There was no question of British soldiers laying down their arms at either of those battles in order to avoid civilian loss of life. In this black and white perspective, the imperative of waging war must always prevail.

In coming to the decision to prosecute, the contrast between the heroism displayed by many battalions during the fighting retreat from Mons and the behaviour of Elkington and Mainwaring at St Quentin must have been the critical factor. Only one standard of behaviour would pass the required test. Only one version of the retreat from Mons could be allowed to prevail. There can be no doubting the fact that, despite all the difficulties and uncertainties, the retreat was conducted bravely and successfully. The BEF lived to fight another day and the tide of battle was eventually turned. But what is equally clear, however, is that Elkington was a superb soldier and a courageous man. His momentary lapse of judgement at St Quentin was just that. It cannot be taken as a fair reflection of his qualities, which were numerous. For Elkington, the verdict of history is clear. He died a soldier, with his reputation for gallantry and service fully intact. Mainwaring died in obscurity. Although he was remembered as a soldier at his death, the cloud of ignominy would never for him be truly lifted, the stain on his character never fully expunged. Whether it was deserved remains very much a matter of controversy.

VC Winners, 23 August–1 September 1914

Maurice Dease, Royal Fusiliers, Mons, 23 August 1914.

Charles Garforth, 15 Hussars, Harmingnies, 23 August 1914.

Sid Godley, Royal Fusiliers, Mons, 23 August 1914.

Charles Jarvis, Royal Engineers, Jemappes, 23 August 1914.

Theodore Wright, Royal Engineers, Mons, 23 August 1914.

Ernest Alexander, Royal Field Artillery, Audregnies, 24 August 1914.

Francis Grenfell, 9 Lancers, Audregnies, 24 August 1914.

George Wyatt, Coldstream Guards, Landrecies, 25/26 August 1914.

Job Drain, Royal Field Artillery, Le Cateau, 26 August 1914.

Fred Holmes, King's Own Yorkshire Light Infantry, Le Cateau, 26 August 1914.

Fred Luke, Royal Field Artillery, Le Cateau, 26 August 1914.

Douglas Reynolds, Royal Field Artillery, Le Cateau, 26 August 1914.

Charles Yate, King's Own Yorkshire Light Infantry, Le Cateau, 26 August 1914.

Edward Bradbury, Royal Horse Artillery, Nery, 1 September 1914.

George Dorrell, Royal Horse Artillery, Nery, 1 September 1914.

David Nelson, Royal Horse Artillery, Nery, 1 September 1914.

Operation Order no. 8

OPERATION ORDER No. 8

BY

FIELD-MARSHAL SIR JOHN FRENCH, G.C.B., ETC.,
Commanding British Expeditionary Force.

G.H.Q.
25/8/1914.

1. The enemy followed our movement this morning and is also passing troops of all arms to the West and South.

2. It is the intention of the C.-in-C. to continue the retirement to-morrow with a view to covering his advanced base and protect his L. of C.

3. For this movement the 19th Brigade will be taken from the Cavalry Division and placed under the orders of the II. Army.

4. The retirement will be carried out from left to right.

5. The 4th Div. will fall back on the western flank in the general direction of Péronne, the western column moving along the line indicated roughly by the line Seranvillers—Le Catelet.

   The movement to commence at 7 A.M.

   The billeting area for to-morrow night being around Le Catelet—Beaurevoir.

   Boundary roads for this force being :

On the East.

   Fontaine — Ligny — Caullery—Elincourt—Serain—Beaurevoir inclus.

On the West.

   Such roads as the G.O.C. 4th Div. wishes to use.

   The II. Corps, with the 19th Bde., will move in echelon and fall back in the general direction of Beaurevoir — Prémont — La Sablière.

   Boundary roads for this force :

On the West.

   Fontaine — Ligny—Caullery—Elincourt—Serain—Beaurevoir exclus.

On the East.

   All roads between the above and the Le Cateau—Busigny road exclusive.

The billeting area for to-morrow night being from Beaurevoir (exclus.) to La Sablière.

7. The I. Corps will start at 5.30 A.M. and march to the area of Busigny, and connect with the II. Corps at La Sablière.

The I. Corps can use the Le Cateau—Busigny road and roads to the East.

Billeting area in Busigny and to the N. and E.

8. The Cav. Div., with the 5th Cav. Bde. attached, will cover the movement on the N. and W. and will arrange their billets outside those already allotted.

9. G.H.Q. to St. Quentin at 7 P.M. to-night.

A. J. Murray,
Lieut.-General,
C.G.S.

Issued at 4 P.M.[1]

---

[1] The II. Corps War Diary states that G.H.Q. Operation Order 8 was received about 9 P.M. Two copies of the order were preserved as appendices to this diary; of these one bears no time of issue, and the other is marked " Issued at 4 P.M." like the G.H.Q. copy, and also the I. Corps copy.

The 4th Division copy of the order is marked " Issued at 7.30 P.M." This is no doubt the correct time. That the time was later than 3.45 P.M. is proved by the following autograph letter from the Sub-Chief of the General Staff to Sir Horace Smith-Dorrien preserved in the G.H.Q. G.S. War Diary :

25th/8/14
3.45 P.M.

Dear Sir Horace,

The C.-in-C. has decided to continue the retirement to-morrow, the left (probably the 4th Division) being directed towards Péronne.

He told me to let you have this private note of his intention.

Orders will follow as soon as the details can be worked out.

v. s. yrs.

Henry Wilson.

4 Division Order of Battle

10 Infantry Brigade
1st Bn Royal Warwickshire Regiment
2nd Bn Seaforth Highlanders
1st Bn Princess Victoria's (Royal Irish Regiment)
2nd Bn Royal Dublin Fusiliers

11 Infantry Brigade
1st Bn Prince Albert's (Somerset Light Infantry)
1st Bn East Lancashire Regiment
1st Bn Hampshire Regiment
1st Bn Rifle Brigade

12 Infantry Brigade
1st Bn King's Own (Royal Lancaster) Regiment
2nd Bn Lancashire Fusiliers
2nd Bn Royal Inniskilling Fusiliers
2nd Bn Essex Regiment

Divisional Mounted Troops – not deployed by 26 August
B Sqn, 19th Hussars
4th Cyclist Company

Artillery
(Units in brackets not deployed by 26 August)
XIV Brigade, Royal Field Artillery:
39th, 68th and 88th Batteries, XIV Brigade Artillery Column

XXIX Brigade, Royal Field Artillery:
125th, 126th and 127th Batteries, XXIX Brigade Artillery Column

XXXII Brigade, Royal Field Artillery:
27th, 134th and 135th Batteries, XXXII Brigade Artillery Column

XXXVII (Howitzer) Brigade, Royal Field Artillery:
31st, 35th and 55th (Howitzer) Batteries, XXXVII (Howitzer) Brigade
    Artillery Column
(31st Heavy Battery, Royal Garrison Artillery and Heavy Artillery Column)
(4th Division Artillery Column)

Colonel Elkington's Interview with the *Daily Sketch*, 8 September 1916

'Colonel Elkington?' John Ford Elkington, late of the Foreign Legion, looked up from his morning paper almost surprised to hear his old title. I had called on him at his delightful old English home in Berkshire today, just as he had read the official announcement that the King had 'approved …'.

A smile lit up the Colonel's face – the smile of a man who had made good – as Mrs Elkington who came into the room at that moment looked as happy as the proud wife of a gallant soldier can look. Colonel Elkington's two children know only that their daddy has come back from the war and that everybody seems to be shaking his hand, ringing him up on the telephone or sending him telegrams that make him glad.

Thinner than he used to be and still suffering from wounds received primarily because of his utter disregard of personal safety when duty called, the Colonel looked every inch a British officer. Wiry and as hard as nails, he made an ideal ranker in that corps of strange men in which rigid discipline, pluck and almost super-human endurance are the things that matter. Colonel Elkington joined the Foreign Legion as an English gentleman who had made a 'mistake'; he was ready to bear the consequences, but anxious to redeem his reputation. 'There is still the Foreign Legion' he said when, by a sentence of a general court martial, he was cashiered early in the war. 'Let's see, when did the war break out? It seems so long ago,' he said to me today. 'August 1914,' I reminded him. 'Then I joined the Foreign Legion in January 1915,' he said.

But about his experiences, Colonel Elkington was reticent. 'I did nothing of particular note,' he said. 'I was with the others in the trenches. Yes, I did what everybody else did at Arras and in the Champagne. We all fought as hard as we could. That's why men join, isn't it?' Not a word did the Colonel say about being noticed by his officers for conspicuously gallant work. No mention did he make of his medals. It was not Colonel Elkington but a friend of his who told me that his bravery in the field in the Champagne caused him to be mentioned in dispatches and the Colonel was sorry I knew so much. He was awarded the Medal Militaire and the Croix de Guerre with palm. And the latter is the highest award a man in the French Army can win. In the Champagne fighting, this man of middle age was wounded. For nearly a year he lay in a French hospital with his right leg shattered, but to his joy, amputation was not necessary. Today he walked with me in the grounds of Purley Hall and with a stick in each hand he can get about with comparative ease. But later in the day he was glad to use his car to respond to an invitation from quite nearby.

'My leg is troublesome, of course,' he said 'and that shot rendered me useless to such a corps as the Foreign Legion. So I came back last Sunday.'

Colonel Elkington has come home in a military sense and only a soldier can understand all that that means to him. He returns to the Royal Warwickshire Regiment in which he was gazetted a Lieutenant in January 1886, Captain nine years later and Major in 1901. The Colonel fought in the Boer War and when he came back he was entitled to wear the Queen's Medal with four clasps for conspicuous service. But Colonel Elkington does not want to wear medals. He has longed to wear his King's uniform again, and his King has asked him to do so.

Colonel Elkington's interview with *The Times*, 9 September 1916

Lieutenant Colonel Elkington, restored to his rank for his gallant service in the Foreign Legion of France, is back again in his old home. Yesterday evening he was sitting by an open window looking out over the gardens through a green vista of trees to where his own sleek cattle were grazing. The voices of his children came up from the lower garden and while he talked to me he listened as does a man who is not quite sure that he may not wake up and find that he has been dreaming. He is back again in his old home, smoking a briar that has been waiting two years untouched on the mantel shelf in the big, panelled room and he wears his old comfortable clothes again.

Colonel Elkington does not understand what he calls 'the fuss' that is being made of him. 'What else could a man do?' he says. 'I was cashiered and after about a fortnight after the notice appeared in the papers I was in the ranks of the Foreign Legion.'

'Under your own name?' I asked. 'Why, of course,' he replied, 'it would not have done for me to have taken another man's name. It was hard work and we were nearly always in the thick of it. I had to take things as they came and three weeks after I had enlisted I was at the front. It was not new to me and I did not need training. Many of the men of the Legion wore medals – medals of all the wars for the last 30 years. I could not wear mine even if I had wanted to and had no right to wear them any longer.'

'Were you ever recognised?' I asked. 'Once only,' he said. 'We were marching in the Champagne country and had just stopped to drink at a stream when a military motor went by. Someone in the car called out "hullo Elkington" and I was afraid I would be given away.'

It was the only voice from the past that came to him and he took it as such. A few minutes afterwards he was stepping it out heel and toe along the dusty road, a private in the Legion.

At a chance reference to Kipling his face lit up. A friend of his sent him a copy of Kipling's 'If'. He carried it in his pack on many a long march through France and it was with him in every attack. He read it in bivouac and in the trenches and he says now emphatically 'it pulled me through the bad times'.

'There was an American with me called Wheeler – a famous surgeon. He came over and joined the French Red Cross. He had tired of that and joined the Legion. I met him first marching up to the front. I thought he was a tramp and I expect he thought I was one. When we got to Lyons I went down to have a meal in the big hotel. There I saw the American sitting over a big dinner and he saw me. From that time on we were friends. We saw that neither was a tramp. We marched together, ate together, and became great pals. He was a fine chap and did not know what fear was and helped to make it a lot easier for me. We went into action together and fell together, both shot in the leg. He gave me first aid and looking at my leg said, "I say old man, they will have to take that off." Then he fainted across my leg and hurt me like the devil. But he saved my life. He is home again. He got the Croix de Guerre but was lamed and no use for further service so he was invalided out.'

Colonel Elkington spent ten months in hospital and eight months on his back. This was the Hospital Civil at Grenoble. He could not say enough for the wonderful treatment that was given him there. They fought to save his life and when they had won that fight, they started to save his leg from amputation. The head of the hospital was a Major Tremier, a splendid surgeon, and he operated eight times and finally succeeded in saving the damaged limb. When he was first in hospital neither the patients nor any of the hospital staff knew what he was or what he had done. Elkington himself got an inkling of his good fortune at Christmas when he heard of his recommendation for the Croix de Guerre.

'Perhaps that helped me get better,' he said. 'The medals are over there on the mantel shelf.' I went over to where there were two glass cases hanging on the wall. 'No, not there, those are my father's and my grandfather's.' He showed me the medals and on the ribbon of the cross there was the little bronze palm branch, which doubles the worth of the medal.

When he was wounded, Dr Wheeler gave him a stiff dose of laudanum, but he lay for thirteen hours until he saw a French patrol passing. He was then one hundred yards short of the German second line of trenches, for this was in the Champagne battle on September 28th, when the French made a magnificent advance.

It was difficult to get Colonel Elkington to talk about himself. As his wife says, he has a horror of advertisement and a photographer who ambushed him outside his own lodge gates yesterday made him feel more nervous than he was charging the machine-gun that wounded him. To say he was happy would be to write a platitude. He is the happiest man in England. He is now recuperating and receiving treatment and he hopes that he will soon be able to walk more than the one hundred yards that taxes his strength to the utmost at present.

Notes

1. See Appendix 1.
2. Edward Spiers, 'The Regular Army in 1914', in *A Nation in Arms*, ed. I. Beckett and K. Simpson (Donovan Publishing, 1985).
3. Tom Bridges, *Alarms and Excursions* (Longman Green, 1938), p. 64.
4. Macdonald, *1914* (Penguin, 1987), p. 183.
5. Haldane, 'Shorncliffe Diary', IWM Document Archive, 69/36/1.
6. Haldane, *A Soldier's Saga* (Blackwood, 1948), p. 278.
7. Douglas Haig, *War Diaries and Letters*, ed. Gary Sheffield and John Bourne (Weidenfeld & Nicholson, 2005), p. 181.
8. National Archives [NA], CAB 45/129, Snow, 'Account of the Retreat of 1914', pp. 3–4.
9. Ibid, p. 4.
10. Edmonds Papers, Liddell Hart Centre for Military Archives, King's College, London.
11. Sir James Edmonds, *Official History of the War, Volume One. Military Operations in France and Belgium, 1914* (Macmillan, 1922), p. 4.
12. Nikolas Gardner, *Trial by Fire* (Praeger, 2003).
13. Edmonds, *Official History*, p. 10.
14. Nigel Hamilton, *Monty: The Making of a General* (Hamish Hamilton, 1981), p. 64.
15. Private R. Hill, in Lewis, *True World War 1 Stories* (Robinson, 1999), p. 10.
16. Haldane, *A Brigade of the Old Army, 1914* (Edward Arnold, 1920), p.1.
17. Private R. Hill, in *True World War 1 Stories*, p. 10.
18. Bridges, *Alarms and Excursions*, p. 75.
19. Montgomery, *Memoirs* (Collins, 1958), pp. 31–2.
20. NA, CAB 45/129, Snow, 'Account of the Retreat'.
21. IWM Private Papers, 6535, Captain Pusey.
22. Private R. Hill, in *True World War 1 Stories*, p. 10.
23. NA, CAB 45/129, Snow, 'Account of the Retreat'.
24. *Irish Life*, 24 September 1914.
25. Bridges, *Alarms and Excursions*, p. 76.
26. NA, CAB 45/129, Snow, 'Account of the Retreat'.
27. Quoted in John Terraine, *Mons. Retreat to Victory* (Wordsworth Military Library, 1960), p. 83.

28. Ibid.
29. IWM Sound Archive, 9339, Corporal Holbrooke.
30. Terraine, *Mons. Retreat to Victory*, p. 84.
31. IWM Sound Archive, 9434, Sergeant Collins.
32. IWM Sound Archive, 188, Sergeant White.
33. Bridges, *Alarms and Excursions*, p. 77.
34. NA, CAB 45/196, Captain Hart.
35. Private R. Hill, in *True World War 1 Stories*.
36. *Irish Life*, 24 September 1914.
37. Mainwaring's statement.
38. Haldane, 'Shorncliffe Diary'.
39. Ibid.
40. Ibid.
41. Ibid.
42. David Ascoli, *The Mons Star* (Birlinn, 2001), p. 79.
43. Quoted in Ascoli, *The Mons Star*, p. 82.
44. Edmonds, *Official History*, p. 102.
45. Bridges, *Alarms and Excursions*, pp. 81–2.
46. Ibid, p. 82.
47. Edmonds, *Official History*, p. 106.
48. J.C. Dunn, *The War the Infantry Knew* (Abacus, 1987), p. 21.
49. Private R. Hill, in *True World War 1 Stories*.
50. NA, CAB 45/129, Snow, 'Account of the Retreat'.
51. IWM Private Papers, 6535, Captain Pusey.
52. NA, CAB 45/196, Captain Hart.
53. NA, CAB 45/197, Lieutenant Macky.
54. NA, CAB 45/129, Snow, 'Account of the Retreat'.
55. Private R. Hill, in *True World War 1 Stories*, p. 11.
56. John Terraine, *General Jack's Diary* (Cassell, 1964), p. 31.
57. Dunn, *The War the Infantry Knew*, pp. 22–3.
58. IWM Sound Archive, 4178, Lieutenant Money.
59. Terraine, *General Jack's Diary*, p. 31.
60. IWM, 4788/80/23/1, Lieutenant Owens.
61. *Irish Life*, 24 September 1914.
62. Haldane, *A Soldier's Saga*, p. 281.
63 NA, CAB 45/129, Snow, 'Account of the Retreat'.
64. Dunn, *The War the Infantry Knew*, p. 23.
65. Terraine, *General Jack's Diary*, p. 32.
66. IWM, 4788/80/23/1, Lieutenant Owens.
67. IWM Sound Archive, 4004, Corporal Atkinson.
68. Haldane, *A Soldier's Saga*, p. 281.
69. NA, WO 95/1477, Haldane's report to Snow.
70. Ibid.

71. Haldane, *A Brigade of the Old Army*, p. 18.
72. NA, CAB 45/129, Snow, 'Account of the Retreat'.
73. NA, CAB 45/196, Captain Hart.
74. NA, CAB 45/129, Snow, 'Account of the Retreat'.
75. Haldane, *A Brigade of the Old Army*, p. 17.
76. NA, WO 95/1482, Captain Clarke.
77. NA, CAB 45/197, Lieutenant Macky.
78. NA, CAB 45/129, Snow, 'Account of the Retreat'.
79. Lord Edward Gleichen, *Infantry Brigade, 1914* (Leonaur Ltd, 2007).
80. Operation Order no. 8, appendix 2.
81. IWM Sound Archive, 4023, Burchmore.
82. Charteris, *At GHQ* (Cassell, 1931), p. 17.
83. Haig, *War Diaries and Letters*, p. 55.
84. Charteris, *At GHQ*, p. 136.
85. See Robin Neillands, *The Old Contemptibles* (John Murray, 2004), p. 116.
86. Bridges, *Alarms and Excursions*, p. 80.
87. Edmonds, *Official History*.
88. NA, CAB 45/206, Smith-Dorrien.
89. Quoted in Ascoli, *The Mons Star*, p. 96.
90. IWM Sound Archive, 4073, Major Davis RA.
91. IWM Sound Archive, 9339, Corporal Holbrooke.
92. IWM Sound Archive, 188, Sergeant White.
93. IWM Private Papers, 6481, Lance-Corporal Botting.
94. IWM Sound Archive, 4004, Corporal Atkinson.
95. IWM Sound Archive, 4178, Lieutenant Money.
96. Ascoli, *The Mons Star*, p. 98.
97. Terraine, *Mons. Retreat to Victory*, p. 131.
98. Haldane, *A Brigade of the Old Army*, pp. 19–20.
99. Ibid.
100. NA, CAB 45/129, Snow, 'Account of the Retreat'.
101. NA, CAB 45/196, Captain Hart.
102. Haldane, *A Brigade of the Old Army*, p. 20.
103. Montgomery, *Memoirs*, p. 32.
104. NA, CAB 45/196, Captain Hart.
105. Private R. Hill, in *True World War 1 Stories*, p. 12.
106. Edmonds, *Official History*, p. 155.
107. NA, WO 95/1477, War Diary of the Royal Dublin Fusiliers, Captain Watson.
108. Ibid, Captain Wheeler.
109. Ibid, War Diary.
110. Ibid, Captain Wheeler.
111. Ibid, Captain Watson.
112. NA, CAB 45/129, Snow, 'Account of the Retreat'.

113. NA, WO 95/1439, Captain Frankland.
114. NA, WO 95/1482, Captain Clarke.
115. NA, CAB 45/196, Captain Hart.
116. NA, CAB 45/197, Lieutenant Macky.
117. John Terraine, *Mons. Retreat to Victory*, p. 139.
118. NA, CAB 45/129, Snow, 'Account of the Retreat'.
119. IWM, Private Papers, 6535, Captain Pusey.
120. Ibid.
121. Private R. Hill, in *True World War 1 Stories*, pp. 12–13.
122. Haldane, *A Brigade of the Old Army*, p. 22.
123. NA, WO 95/1477, Haldane.
124. Ibid.
125. Ibid.
126. IWM, Private Papers, 592, Lieutenant Butt.
127. Ibid.
128. IWM, Private Papers, 3762, Sergeant Spencer.
129. IWM Sound Archive, 4004, Corporal Atkinson.
130. Fred Petch, quoted in Ascoli, *The Mons Star*, p. 105.
131. IWM Sound Archive, 4169, Lieutenant MacLeod.
132. Jack Tyrell, quoted in Ascoli, *The Mons Star*, p. 103.
133. Dunn, *The War the Infantry Knew*, p. 29, Major Geiger.
134. Ibid. Regimental Sergeant-Major Boreham.
135. NA, CAB 45/206, Smith-Dorrien.
136. NA, CAB 45/129, Snow, 'Account of the Retreat'.
137. Ibid.
138. WO 45/1439.
139. Private R. Hill, in *True World War I Stories*, p. 13.
140. Edmonds, *Official History*, p. 180.
141. NA, CAB 45/129, Snow, 'Account of the Retreat'.
142. See Appendix 2.
143. NA, WO 95/1477, Captain Watson.
144. Ibid, Captain Wheeler.
145. NA, WO 95/1484, Major Poole.
146. Ibid.
147. NA, CAB 45/196, Captain Hart.
148. NA, WO 95/1477, Haldane.
149. Haldane, *A Soldier's Saga*, pp. 27-8.
150. NA, CAB 45/129, Snow, 'Account of the Retreat'.
151. Ibid, p. 281.
152. Ibid.
153. Ibid.
154. Edmonds, *Official History*, p. 182.
155. Sir John French, *1914* (Constable, 1919).

156. NA, CAB 45/129, Snow, 'Account of the Retreat'.
157. Edmonds, *Official History*, p. 191–2.
158. NA, CAB 45/129, Snow, 'Account of the Retreat'.
159. Private R. Hill, in *True World War 1 Stories*, p. 12.
160. IWM Sound Archive, 9434, Sergeant Collins.
161. Dunn, *The War the Infantry Knew*, p. 30.
162. NA, CAB 45/206, Smith-Dorrien.
163. IWM 3762 85/43/1, Gunner Bellow.
164. Bridges, *Alarms and Excursions*, p. 85.
165. Ibid.
166. Harold Gibb, *Record of the 4th Dragoon Guards in the Great War, 1914–18* (Canterbury, 1925), p. 11.
167. Arthur Osburn, *Unwilling Passenger* (Faber & Faber, 1932), p. 78.
168. IWM Sound Archive, 9434, Sergeant Collins.
169. IWM Sound Archive, 9339, Corporal Holbrooke.
170. Dunn, *The War the Infantry Knew*, p. 31.
171. Bridges, *Alarms and Excursions*, p. 86.
172. Private R. Hill, in *True World War I Stories*, p. 13.
173. Bridges, *Alarms and Excursions*, p. 85.
174. Ibid, p. 87.
175. Ibid, p. 87.
176. Osburn, *Unwilling Passenger*, p. 79.
177. Bridges, *Alarms and Excursions*, p. 87.
178. Ibid, pp. 83-4.
179. Ibid, pp. 87–8.
180. NA, WO 95/1477, War Diary of 10th Infantry Brigade.
181. British Library, Hunter Weston Papers 48363.
182. Ibid.
183. Gardner, *Trial by Fire*, p. 17.
184. NA, CAB 45/129, Snow, 'Account of the Retreat'.
185. *Manual of Military Law* (HMSO, 1914), p. 380.
186. Richard van Emden, *'Tickled to Death to Go': Memoirs of a Cavalryman* (History Press, 1996).
187. British Library, Hunter Weston Papers, 48363.
188. Ibid, 48365.
189. Bridges, *Alarms and Excursions*, p. 86.
190. NA, CAB 45/129, Snow, 'Account of the Retreat'.
191. Ibid.
192. Service historique de l'Armee de terre, 7N 1287, Paris.
193. Russell Kelly, *Kelly of the Foreign Legion* (New York, Mitchell Kennerley, 1917), p. 46.
194. See Peter Scott, *Dishonoured. The Colonels Surrender at St Quentin* (Tom Donovan, 1994), p. 70 and John Ashby, *Seek Glory Now Keep Glory* (Helion & Company, 2000), p. 96.

195. See Appendix 5.
196. *The Times*, 6 September 1916.
197. Blaise Cendrars, *La main coupee* (Paris, Folio, 1974).
198. Hugh McLeave, *The Damned Die Hard* (Saxon House, 1974), pp. 125-6.
199. David Wooster King, *An Intimate Story of the Foreign Legion* (New York, Duffield, 1927), p. 18.
200. Bridges, *Alarms and Excursions*, p. 88.
201. John Parker, *Inside the Foreign Legion* (Piatkus, 1998), p. 61.
202. Handwritten note in NA, WO 90/6/28, recording the king's decision to reinstate Elkington's rank.
203. *Newbury Weekly News*, 23 May 1946.

Bibliography

Ascoli, David, *The Mons Star* (Birlinn, 1981).

Ashby, John, *Seek Glory Now Keep Glory* (Helion & Company, 2000).

Battle of Le Cateau, 26th August 1914. Tour of the Battlefield (HMSO, 1934).

Beckett, I., and Simpson, K., *A Nation in Arms* (Donovan Publishing, 1985).

Bridges, Tom, *Alarms and Excursions* (Longmans, 1938).

Brown, Malcolm, *The IWM Book of 1914. The Men Who Went to War* (Sidgwick & Jackson, 2004).

Charteris, J., *At GHQ* (Cassell, 1931).

Dunn, J.C., *The War the Infantry Knew, 1914–1919* (Abacus, 1994).

Edmonds, Sir James, *Official History of the War Volume One. Military Operations in France and Belgium, 1914* (Macmillan, 1922).

Haig, Douglas, *War Diaries and Letters*, ed. Gary Sheffield and John Bourne (Weidenfeld & Nicholson, 2005).

Haldane, Sir Aylmer, *A Brigade of the Old Army, 1914* (Edward Arnold, 1920).

Haldane, Sir Aylmer, *A Soldier's Saga* (Blackwood, 1948).

Holmes, Richard, *Tommy* (HarperCollins, 2004).

Gardner, Nikolas, *Trial by Fire* (Praeger Publishers, 2003).

Gibb, Revd Harold, *Record of the 4th Irish Dragoon Guards, 1914–18* (Canterbury, privately printed, 1925).

Gleichen, Lord Edward, *Infantry Brigade, 1914* (Leonaur, 2007).

King, David W., *An Intimate Story of the Foreign Legion* (New York, Duffield, 1927).

Macdonald, Lyn, *1914. The Days of Hope* (Penguin, 1987).

McLeave, Hugh, *The Damned Die Hard* (Saxon House, 1974).

Montgomery, B.L., *Memoirs* (Collins, 1958).

Neillands, Robin, *The Old Contemptibles* (John Murray, 2004).

Osburn, Arthur, *Unwilling Passenger* (Faber & Faber, 1932).

Parker, John, *Inside the Foreign Legion* (Piatkus, 1998).

Porch, Douglas, *The French Foreign Legion* (Macmillan, 1991).

Scott, Peter, *Dishonoured. The Colonels Surrender at St Quentin* (Tom Donovan, 1994).

Terraine, John, *General Jack's Diary* (Cassell, 1964).

Terraine, John, *Mons. Retreat to Victory* (Wordsworth Editions, 1960).

Wylly, Colonel H.C., *Crown and Company. The Historical Records of the 2nd Battalion, Royal Dublin Fusiliers, Vol. 2, 1911–22* (G&P, 1923).

National Archive Material

CAB 45/206 Papers of General Sir H. Smith-Dorrien.

CAB 45/129: Personal papers of General Sir Thomas d'Oyly Snow, including his 'Account of the Retreat of 1914'.

CAB 45/196: Captain H.C. Hart's account of the days leading up to and including the battle of Le Cateau.

CAB 45/197: Lieutenant Macky's account of the events surrounding the battle of Le Cateau.

WO 95/1439: War Diary of the 4th Division, BEF.

WO 95/1477: War Diary of the 10th Infantry Brigade, including personal accounts of the retreat from Le Cateau by General Haldane, Major Poole and Captains Frankland, Watson and Wheeler.

WO 95/1482: War Diary of the 2nd Battalion, Royal Dublin Fusiliers.

WO 95/1484: War Diary of the 1st Battalion, Royal Warwickshire Regiment.

Index

The names of Colonel John Ford Elkington and Colonel Arthur Edward Mainwaring have not been indexed, as they occur *passim*. References in italics are to illustrative material.